AN INTRODUCTION TO OPTIONS TRADING

The Securities & Investment Institute

Mission Statement:

> *To set standards of professional excellence and integrity for the investment and securities industry, providing qualifications and promoting the highest level of competence to our members, other individuals and firms.*

The Securities and Investment Institute is the UK's leading professional and membership body for practitioners in the securities and investment industry, with more than 16,000 members with an increasing number working outside the UK. It is also the major examining body for the industry, with a full range of qualifications aimed at people entering and working in it. More than 30,000 examinations are taken annually in more than 30 countries.

You can contact us through our website *www.sii.org.uk*

Our membership believes that keeping up to date is central to professional development. We are delighted to endorse the Wiley/SII publishing partnership and recommend this series of books to our members and all those who work in the industry.

As part of the SII CPD Scheme, reading relevant financial publications earns members of the Securities & Investment Institute the appropriate number of CPD hours under the Self-Directed learning category. For further information, please visit *www.sii.org.uk/cpdscheme*

Ruth Martin
Managing Director

AN INTRODUCTION TO OPTIONS TRADING

....

Frans de Weert

JOHN WILEY & SONS, LTD

Copyright © 2006   John Wiley & Sons Ltd, The Atrium, Southern Gate, Chichester,
West Sussex PO19 8SQ, England

Telephone (+44) 1243 779777

Email (for orders and customer service enquiries): cs-books@wiley.co.uk
Visit our Home Page on www.wiley.com

Reprinted December 2006

Other Wiley Editorial Offices

John Wiley & Sons, Inc., 111 River Street, Hoboken, NJ 07030, USA

Jossey-Bass, 989 Market Street, San Francisco, CA 94103-1741, USA

Wiley-VCH Verlag GmbH, Boschstr. 12, D-69469 Weinheim, Germany

John Wiley & Sons Australia Ltd, 42 McDougall Street, Milton, Queensland 4064, Australia

John Wiley & Sons (Asia) Pte Ltd, 2 Clementi Loop #02-01, Jin Xing Distripark, Singapore 129809

John Wiley & Sons Canada Ltd, 6045 Freemont Blvd, Mississauga, Ontario, Canada L5R 4J3

Wiley also publishes its books in a variety of electronic formats. Some content that appears
in print may not be available in electronic books.

British Library Cataloguing in Publication Data

A catalogue record for this book is available from the British Library

ISBN-13 978-0-470-02970-1 (PB)

Project management by Originator, Gt Yarmouth, Norfolk (typeset in 12/16pt Trump Mediaeval).
Printed and bound in Great Britain by T.J. International Ltd, Padstow, Cornwall.
This book is printed on acid-free paper responsibly manufactured from sustainable forestry
in which at least two trees are planted for each one used for paper production.

To Jan and Annelies

CONTENTS

....

Appendices

PREFACE

· ·

This book is appropriate for people who want to get a good overview of options in practice. It especially deals with hedging of options and how option traders earn money by doing so. To point out where the profit of option traders comes from, common terms in option theory will be explained, and it is shown how they relate to this profit. The use of mathematics is restricted to a minimum. However, since mathematics makes it possible to lift analyses to a non-superficial level, mathematics is used to clarify and generalize certain phenomena.

The aim of this book is to give both option practitioners as well as interested individuals the necessary tools to deal with options in practice. Throughout this book real life examples will illustrate why investors use option structures to satisfy their needs. Although understanding the contents of this book is a prerequisite for becoming a good option practitioner, a book can never produce a good trader. Ninety percent of a trader's job is about dealing with severe losses and still being able to make the right decisions if such a loss occurs. The only way to become a good trader is to accept that, when helping clients to execute their option strategies, the trader will inevitably end up with positions where the risk reward is against him but the odds are in his favour. For that reason a one-off loss will almost always be larger than a one-off gain. But, if a trader executes many deals he should be able to make money on the small margin he collects on every deal even if he gets a few blow-ups.

ACKNOWLEDGEMENTS

. . . .

This book is based on knowledge acquired during my work as a trader at Barclays Capital. Therefore, I would like to thank my colleagues at Barclays Capital who have been very helpful in teaching me the theory and practice of options. At Barclays Capital I would especially like to thank Faisal Khan and Thierry Lucas for giving me all the opportunities to succeed in mastering and practising option trading. I would also like to thank Thierry Lucas for his many suggestions and corrections when reviewing my work and Alex Boer for his mathematical insights. I would especially like to thank Karma Dajani for first giving me a great foundation in probability theory, then supervising my graduate dissertation in mathematics and, lastly, reviewing this book. Special thanks goes out to my father, Jan de Weert, for having been a motivating and helpful force in mastering mathematics throughout my life, and for checking the book very thoroughly and giving me many suggestions in rephrasing sentences and formulae more clearly.

INTRODUCTION

. . . .

Over the years derivative securities have become increasingly important. Examples of these are options, futures, forwards and swaps. Although every derivative has its own purpose, they all have in common that their values depend on more basic variables like stocks and interest rates. This book is only concerned with options, but once the theory behind options is known, knowledge can easily be expanded to other derivatives.

This book has three objectives. The first is to introduce terms commonly used in option theory and explain their practical interpretation. The second is to show where option traders get their profit and how these commonly used terms relate to this profit. The last objective is to show why companies and investors use options to satisfy their financial needs.

Chapter

1

· ·

OPTIONS

Options on stocks were first traded on an organized exchange in 1973. That very same year Black and Scholes introduced their famous Black–Scholes formula. This formula gives the price of an option in terms of its parameters, like the underlying asset, time to maturity and interest rate. The formula and the variables it depends on will be discussed in more detail in the next chapters. Since 1973 option markets have grown rapidly, not only in volumes but also in the range of option products to be traded. Nowadays, options can be traded on many different exchanges throughout the world and on many different underlying assets. These underlying assets include stocks, stock indices, currencies and commodities.

There are two general kinds of options, the *call option* and the *put option*. A call option gives the holder the right, **but not the obligation**, to buy the underlying asset for a pre-specified price and at a pre-specified date. A put option gives the holder the right, **but not the obligation**, to sell the underlying asset for a pre-specified price and at a pre-specified date. This pre-specified price is called the 'strike price'; the date is known as the 'expiration date', or 'maturity'. The underlying asset in the definition of an option can be virtually anything, like potatoes, the weather, or stocks. Throughout this book the underlying asset will be taken to be a stock.

When the owner of a call option chooses to buy the stock, it is said that he exercises his option right. Of course, the same holds for the owner of a put option, only in this case the owner chooses to sell the stock, but it is still referred to as 'exercising' the option. If the option can only be exercised on the expiration date itself, the option is said to be a 'European' option. If it can be exercised at any time up to expiration, the option is an 'American' option. Although there are many other option types, the most important ones have already been covered: American call option, American put option, European call option and the European put option. The vast majority of the options that are traded on exchanges are American. However, it is useful to analyze European options, because properties of American options can very often be deduced from its European counterpart.

Before an example is given, it is worthwhile to look at the boldface sentence in the definition of an option. The holder of an option is not obligated to exercise the option. This means that at maturity the holder can decide not to do anything. This is exactly why it is called an 'option', the holder has a choice of doing something. Because of this choice, the largest loss an owner of an option can face is the price paid for the option.

1.1   EXAMPLES

Consider a holder of a European call option on the stock Royal Dutch/Shell with a strike price of $42. Suppose that the current stock price is $40, the expiration date is in 1 year and the option price is $5. Since the option is European, it can only be exercised on the expiration date. What are the possible payoffs for this option? If on the expiration date the stock price is less than $42, the holder of this option will clearly not exercise his option right.

For if he did, he would buy the stock for $42 (exercising the option), and would only be able to sell the stock on the market for less than $42. So, the holder would incur a loss if he exercised his right, whereas nothing would happen if he did not exercise this right. In conclusion, if on the expiration date the stock price is less than $42, the holder does not exercise the option. In these circumstances the holder's loss is the price paid for the option, in this case $5. If on the expiration date the stock price is between $42 and $47, the holder will exercise his option right. Suppose that the stock price on the expiration date is $45, then, by exercising his option right, he buys the stock for $42 and immediately sells this stock on the market for $45, making a profit of $3. However, taking into account that he paid $5 for the option, he still makes a loss of $2. It is clear that up to $47 the holder loses money on the option. If on the expiration date the stock price is more than $47, the holder will again exercise his option right. The difference between this case and the previous one is that the holder not only makes a profit by exercising his option right, he also makes an overall profit. Suppose that the stock price on the expiration date is $49, then his profit is $2, $7 from exercising the option and −$5 from the price paid for the option. Figure 1.1 shows the way in which the profit of the holder of a call option on Royal Dutch/Shell varies with the stock price at maturity.

This example points out that the profit of the holder of a call option increases as the stock price increases. Thus, the holder of a call option is speculating on an increasing stock price.

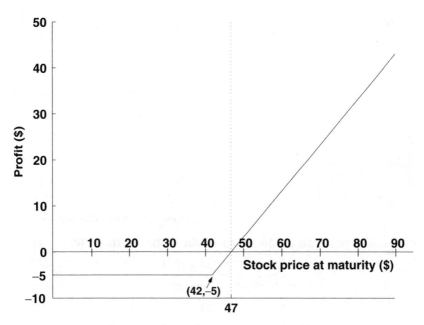

Figure 1.1 Profit from buying a European call option on Royal Dutch/Shell. Option price = $5, Strike price = $42.

In contrast to a call option, the owner of a put option is hoping that the stock price will decrease. Consider a holder of a European put option on Unilever with a strike price of $50. Suppose that the current stock price is $50, the expiration date is in 6 months and the option price is $3. Again, because the put option is European it can only be exercised on the expiration date. What are the possible payoffs for the put option? Suppose that the stock price at maturity (expiration date) is more than $50. In this case the holder would not exercise his option right. Because he would have to buy the stock for more than $50, and, under the conditions of the put options, sell the same stock for $50. This would mean he would always incur a loss. So, if the stock price is more than $50, the holder does not exercise the option and faces a loss of $3, the

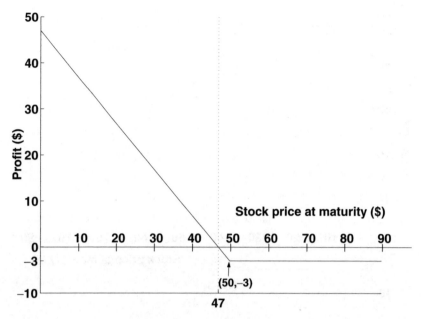

Figure 1.2   Profit from buying a European put option on Unilever.
Option price = $3, Strike price = $50.

price paid for the put option. If the stock price at maturity
is between $50 and $47, the holder will exercise the
option, but still make an overall loss. He will earn money
by exercising the option, but it will not be enough to
make up for the initial $3 paid for the option. If the
stock price is less than $47 at maturity, the holder will
exercise the option, and make an overall profit. He will
make a profit of more than $3 by buying the stock on the
market and immediately selling this stock for $50 under
the conditions of the put option. Since the price paid for
the put option was $3 he will also make an overall profit.
Figure 1.2 shows the way in which the profit of the holder
of the put option on Unilever varies with the stock price
at maturity.

1.2 AMERICAN VERSUS EUROPEAN OPTIONS

If in above examples the options were American rather than European, the holders of the options would not have to wait until the expiration date before exercising the options. In the example of the put option on Unilever with strike price $50 this would mean that at any time during the 6 months, the holder is allowed to exercise the option. So, suppose that after 3 months the stock price is $40, the holder could decide to exercise his option right. By exercising he would make a profit of $7, $10 from exercising the option and −$3 from the price paid for the option.

Everything that can be done with a European option can be done with an American option, but the American option has the additional property that it can be exercised at any time up to the expiration date. This means that its price is always at least as much as its European counterpart.

Although most options that are traded on exchanges are American, this book mainly focuses on European options. Since American options are based on the same principles as European ones, and their properties can, very often, be easily derived from the European counterparts this is perfectly arguable. Throughout this book, an option is assumed to be European, unless specifically stated otherwise.

1.3 TERMINOLOGY

An option contract is an agreement between two parties. The buyer of the option is said to 'have taken a long position' in the option. The other party is said to have taken a 'short position' in the option, or is said to have 'written' the option. So, taking a long position essentially means 'buying' and taking a short position means 'selling'. For that reason there are four general option positions:

1. A short position in a call option.
2. A short position in a put option.
3. A long position in a call option.
4. A long position in a put option.

Although it is tempting to say that positions 1 and 4 are basically the same whenever the options have the same strike price, and also positions 2 and 3, there is one big difference. The short position always bears a greater risk, because losses can be unlimited and profits are bounded. For that reason the party holding a short position gets money from the party holding a long position, which is of course equal to the price of the option. For example, the loss of an investor with a short position in a call option can be unlimited, whereas the loss of an investor with a long position in a call option is bounded by the price of the option. The profit of an investor with a short position in a call option is bounded by the price of the option, and the profit of an investor with a long position in a call option is unlimited. In fact, it is not totally true that losses can be unlimited for investors holding a short position. In

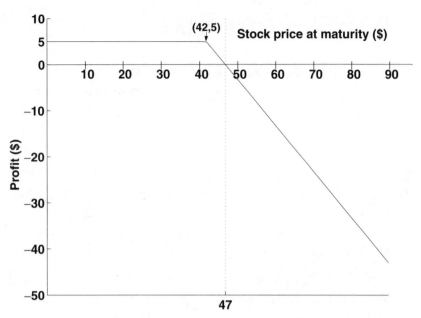

Figure 1.3 Profit from writing a European call option on Royal Dutch/Shell. Option price = $5, Strike price = $42.

the case of a short position in a put option, the losses are bounded by the strike price, since the stock price cannot drop below 0. Respectively, Figures 1.3 and 1.4 show the variation of the profit and loss with the stock price at maturity of an investor holding a short position in a European call option on Royal Dutch/Shell, and an investor holding a short position in a European put option on Unilever. Respectively, when Figures 1.3 and 1.4 are compared with Figures 1.1 and 1.2, it also becomes clear that a short position always bears a greater risk than a long position.

An option has three states, *in the money*, *at the money* and *out of the money*. Every state refers to what would happen were the option exercised immediately. For

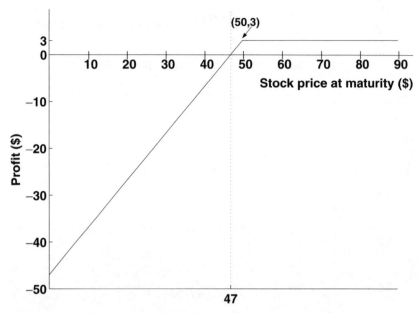

Figure 1.4 Profit from writing a European put option on Unilever. Option price = $3, Strike price = $50.

example, consider the call option on Royal Dutch/Shell with a strike price of $42. If the stock price of Royal Dutch/Shell is more than $42, the call option is in the money, because a profit would be made by exercising the option immediately. The call option is at the money if the stock price is $42, since neither a profit nor a loss would be made by exercising the option immediately. The call option is out of the money if the stock price were less than $42, since by exercising the option immediately the holder would incur a loss. For the put option the reverse holds. A put option is in the money if the strike price is more than the stock price, at the money if the strike price is equal to the stock price and out of the money if the

Table 1.1 States of an option.

Ratio	State call option	State put option
$\dfrac{S_t}{K} = 1 + \dfrac{x}{100} > 1$	$x\%$ in the money	$x\%$ out of the money
$\dfrac{S_t}{K} = 1$	At the money	At the money
$\dfrac{S_t}{K} = 1 - \dfrac{x}{100} < 1$	$x\%$ out of the money	$x\%$ in the money

strike price is less than the stock price. Table 1.1 summarizes the three states of an option.[1]

The *intrinsic* value of an option is the payoff were the option exercised immediately. Consider a call option, with strike price \$40, on a stock with a price of \$50. For this particular option the intrinsic value is \$10. This definition implies that in-the-money options have positive intrinsic values, whereas at-the-money and out-of-the-money options have intrinsic values equal to 0.

Furthermore, it is good to discuss the economic principle of *discounting* here. The easiest way to illustrate this is by means of an example. Consider an option trader who owns a European option with an expiration date in 1 year and an expected payoff at maturity of \$4. One could be tempted to say that the price of this option should be \$4 as well, since in this case both sides of the option contract will have expected profit of 0. However, this is not quite

---

[1] S_t stands for the stock price at time t and K stands for the strike of the option.

true, because the seller of the option gets $4 a year earlier than the buyer of the option. So, in fact the fair price of the option should be that amount of money such that when it is put in a savings account for 1 year it has grown to $4. This means that if the interest rate is 6% per year the fair price is $4/1.06 = \$3.77$. The foregoing is referred to as 'discounting', and in this case $4 is discounted at 6%. In the above calculation it is assumed that interest is paid out only once a year. In practice, it is actually paid out continuously, which implies that money on a savings account grows faster, because interest is paid out on the initial amount plus the interest earned up to that time. In this case the discounting formula is $4 \times e^{-0.06 \times 1}$. In general, if an amount x has to be discounted at an interest rate of r (expressed as a percentage) per year over a period of $T - t$ years, the discounting formula is $x \times e^{-r \times (T-t)}$.

Lastly, it is worth mentioning that it is possible to short (sell) a stock without actually owning it. It basically comes down to borrowing a stock from a third party after which the stock is sold immediately. However, this stock has to be returned sometime. For example, an investor shorts the stock Unilever for $50. Because the investor sells the stock Unilever he gets the $50. If after 1 year the stock price of Unilever is $40 he can decide to buy the stock on the market for $40 and return it to the party he borrowed it from. With this strategy the investor makes a profit of $10 if the interest rate is 0%, and if the interest rate is r (expressed as a percentage) it gives a profit of $50 \times (1 + r) - 40$, or if interest is paid continuously $50 \times e^{r \times 1} - 40$.

1.4 EARLY EXERCISE OF AMERICAN OPTIONS

For a call option on a non-dividend paying stock, it appears that the prices for both European and American types are exactly the same. In other words, it is never optimal to exercise a call option on a non-dividend paying stock early. Because the price of a stock is an expectation of the future earnings there are always investors who want to hold the stock longer than the term of the option. Even if such investors did not care about the option part, they would still be prepared to pay more for an American call option than its intrinsic value, since there is an interest rate advantage. This is because the price of a call option is always less than the price of its underlying stock, otherwise money could be made by buying the stock and shorting the call option. So, for an investor planning to hold the underlying non-dividend paying stock longer than the term of the option, it would be cheaper to buy the call option for its intrinsic value than to actually buy the stock. For that reason this particular investor, which must exist, would be prepared to pay more than just the intrinsic value. Knowing this, it is easy to see why it is never optimal to exercise an American call option on a non-dividend paying stock early. Consider an American call option on Royal Dutch/ Shell with a strike price of $40 and an expiration date in 1 year. Suppose that after half a year the stock price is $50. The holder of this call option could be tempted to exercise his option, getting a payoff of $10.

However, it would be better not to exercise the call option, but to sell the call option instead. Since the price of the option is more than its intrinsic value this would lead to a higher payoff than $10. An alternative strategy[2] is to keep the option and short the underlying stock. This guarantees a payoff of at least $10. On top of that, interest is earned over $50, since this was received by shorting the stock, which is more than the interest earned on the $10 were the American option exercised immediately. This means that the discounted expected payoff is more than $10.

However, for an American put option it can be profitable to exercise the option early. This can be shown by looking at an extreme but simple example.[3] Consider an investor with a put option on Royal Dutch/Shell with a strike price of $40 and an expiration date in 1 year. Now suppose that after half a year Royal Dutch/Shell is virtually worth nothing (very extreme situation). By exercising the put option, the investor makes an immediate gain of $40. If the investor waits, the gain could be less than $40 but it could never be more than $40, since stock prices cannot drop below 0. This already shows that there can be a point in exercising an American put option on a non-dividend paying stock early. Furthermore, receiving $40 now is preferable to receiving $40 in the future (interest rate advantage). It follows that in this case the American put option should be exercised immediately.

---

[2] Argument on p. 158 of Hull (1993).
[3] The following argument is based on pp. 160/161 of Hull (1993).

1.5 PAYOFFS

The examples show that the payoff of an option can never be negative, since the holder can decide not to exercise his option right. This does not mean that the profit of the owner of an option cannot be negative. This is of course because an initial price has been paid for the option. So, a distinction has to be made between the profit of an option and the payoff. The payoff only consists of the cash flow at the time the option is exercised, whereas the profit also takes the price of the option into account. It is easy to actually characterize the payoff of an option at maturity. Suppose that S_T is the price of the underlying stock at maturity, and K is the strike price of the option. The payoff from a long position in a European call option is:

$$\max(S_T - K, 0)$$

This formula is in compliance with the fact that the option will be exercised if $S_T > K$, and will not be exercised if $S_T \leq K$. The payoff from a short position in a European call is:

$$-\max(S_T - K, 0)$$

This is again logical, since whatever the holder of a long position wins by exercising, the holder of a short position loses. So, the payoff for the short position is minus the payoff of the long position. The payoff to a holder of a long position in a European put option is:

$$\max(K - S_T, 0)$$

This formula shows that the put option is exercised if $S_T < K$, and is not exercised if $S_T \geq K$. The short position in a European put option has a payoff of:

$$- \max(K - S_T, 0)$$

1.6 PUT–CALL PARITY

The put–call parity is a relation between the call option price (c_t), the put option price (p_t), the stock price (S_t) and the strike price (K) of the call and put option, provided the strike price and the time to maturity are the same for both the call and the put option. The proof of this put–call parity uses the assumption of absence of arbitrage. Arbitrage means that it is possible to make a profit without running any risk. So, the profit of an arbitrage strategy can never be less than 0 and there is a chance that it makes a positive profit. In practice, the absence of arbitrage assumption is a very reasonable assumption. With this knowledge it is easy to state and prove the put–call parity. When there is absence of arbitrage there exists a put–call parity, given by:

$$c_t - p_t = S_t - K e^{-r(T-t)} \qquad (1.1)$$

where c_t = Price of a European call option with strike price K and a time to maturity of $T - t$;

p_t = Price of a European put option with strike price K and a time to maturity of $T - t$;

S_t = Price of the underlying stock of both the call and the put option at time t;

r = Interest rate expressed as a percentage and in the same unit of time as $T - t$;

K = Strike price.

The put–call parity will be proved by assuming it does not hold and showing that this leads to a contradiction. So, it will be proved in two steps. First, it will be assumed that $c_t - p_t > S_t - K e^{-r(T-t)}$, and showing this leads to an arbitrage possibility. Then, it will be assumed that $c_t - p_t < S_t - K e^{-r(T-t)}$, and showing this also leads to an arbitrage possibility. The fact that both assumptions lead to an arbitrage possibility is a contradiction, because for the put–call parity it was assumed there was absence of arbitrage:

1. Suppose $c_t - p_t > S_t - K e^{-r(T-t)}$, that is:

$$K + e^{r(T-t)}(c_t - p_t - S_t) > 0 \qquad (1.2)$$

By entering in the following portfolio at time t, a profit will always be made at maturity, T.

○ At time t

- long 1 underlying stock   (yield $-S_t$)
- long 1 put option   (yield $-p_t$)
- short 1 call option   (yield c_t)

The total yield of this portfolio is:

$$c_t - p_t - S_t \qquad (1.3)$$

○ At maturity, T

- $K > S_T$
 In this case the call option will not be exercised, but the put will. By exercising the put, the underlying stock in the portfolio will be sold for

K, closing down the portfolio's position. The profit of this portfolio is:

$$K + e^{r(T-t)}(c_t - p_t - S_t) > 0 \qquad (1.4)$$

- $K < S_T$
  The put will not be exercised, but the call will. Because the call is being exercised, the underlying stock in the portfolio will be sold for $K to the holder of the call option, closing down the portfolio's position. The profit of the portfolio is:

$$K + e^{r(T-t)}(c_t - p_t - S_t) > 0 \qquad (1.5)$$

2. Suppose $c_t - p_t < S_t - Ke^{-r(T-t)}$, that is:

$$e^{r(T-t)}(S_t + p_t - c_t) - K > 0 \qquad (1.6)$$

By entering in the following portfolio at time t, a profit will always be made at maturity, T.

o At time t

   - short 1 underlying stock   (yield S_t)
   - short 1 put option   (yield p_t)
   - long 1 call option   (yield -c_t)

The total yield of this portfolio is:

$$S_t + p_t - c_t \qquad (1.7)$$

o At maturity, T

   - $K > S_T$
     In this case the call option will not be exercised,

but the put will. Because the put is being exercised, the underlying stock will be bought for $K from the holder of the put option, closing down the short position in this underlying stock. The profit of this portfolio is:

$$e^{r(T-t)}(S_t + p_t - c_t) - K > 0 \qquad (1.8)$$

– $K < S_T$

The put option will not be exercised, but the call will be exercised. By exercising the call, the underlying stock will be bought for $K, closing down the short position in this underlying stock. The profit of this portfolio is:

$$e^{r(T-t)}(S_t + p_t - c_t) - K > 0 \qquad (1.9)$$

Since both the assumption $c_t - p_t > S_t - Ke^{-r(T-t)}$ as well as $c_t - p_t < S_t - K e^{-r(T-t)}$ lead to an arbitrage possibility, the put–call parity, $c_t - p_t = S_t - K e^{-r(T-t)}$, has to hold.

Chapter

2

THE BLACK–SCHOLES FORMULA

In the previous chapter the definition of an option was given. Furthermore, some examples showed what the payoff and profit of an option look like. In these examples the price of the option was always given. It is however possible to identify what the fair price of a European option should be. In this perspective 'fair' means that the expected profit for both sides of the option contract is 0. The Black–Scholes formula is a good tool for determining the fair price of an option. From the definition of an option it is clear that the price should depend on the strike price, the price of the underlying stock and the time to maturity. It appears that the price of an option also depends on less obvious variables. These other variables are interest rates, the volatility of the underlying stock (the way the stock moves) and the dividends on the stock. By some simple examples it can be clarified that the option price should also depend on the last mentioned variables:

- *Interest rate.* Suppose that the interest rate given on a savings account is 5% per year. Consider a put option with a time to maturity of 1 year, and, given an interest rate of 5%, the price of this option is $10. Since the holder of the short position in this option gets this $10, he can put this money in a savings account, getting a 5% interest rate. By doing so he will have $10.5 $(10 * 1.05)$ at the expiration date of the option. Since the price of the option is fair, the expected payoff for the holder of the long position in the option will also be $10.5. Now suppose that the interest rate was not 5% but 6%. Higher interest rates cause expected growth rates on stocks to increase, otherwise investors in stocks could be tempted to sell their stocks and put the money in a savings account. This means that the expected payoff of a put option is likely to be less. Although this is generally true, suppose that the expected payoff to the holder of the long position does not change and will still be $10.5. The question is: What should the price of the option be in this case? The price should be such that the holder of the short position has $10.5 at maturity. This implies that the price is 10.5 discounted at a rate of 6%. In other words, the price is $9.91 (10.5/1.06). If the effect of increasing expected growth rates on stocks when the interest rate is higher was taken into account, the option price would have been even less. This shows that option prices differ as the interest rate differs. The price of a put option is less if the interest rate is higher, and for a call option the reverse holds. In Section 2.2, this effect will be discussed in more detail. Figure 2.1 shows in which way the prices of an at-the-money call and put option vary with interest rate. Note that if the interest rate is 0 the prices of an at-the-money call and put option are the same, which is perfectly in compliance with the put–call parity. Furthermore, it is worth noticing that the price of an *at-the-money* put option changes faster with interest rate than an *at-the-money* call option. This means that an *at-the-money* put option is more sensitive to interest rate changes than an *at-the-money* call option, which will be discussed in more detail in Section 2.2.

- *Volatility.* Volatility is a complex concept, but in this example a simple definition will be used to clarify the dependence of the option price on volatility. Volatility

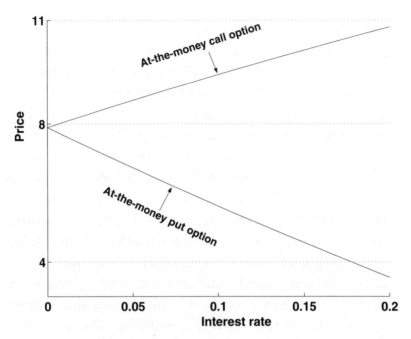

Figure 2.1 Variations of at-the-money call and put option prices with interest rate.

is a variable that measures the movement of a stock. Consider the stock Unilever with a price of $50. If the volatility is 0.1 this means, in this example, that after 1 year the stock price is either $55 or $45. If the volatility is 0.2 this means that after 1 year it is either $60 or $40. Consider a European call option on Unilever with a time to maturity of 1 year. If the volatility of Unilever is 0.1, the expected payoff at maturity is $2.5 $((55 - 50) \times 0.5 + 0 \times 0.5)$. If the volatility of Unilever is 0.2, the expected payoff at maturity is $5 $((60 - 50) \times 0.5 + 0 \times 0.5)$. Since the expected payoff is greater if the volatility is 0.2 than if the volatility is 0.1, the price of the option should be higher if the volatility is 0.2. In general, the higher the volatility

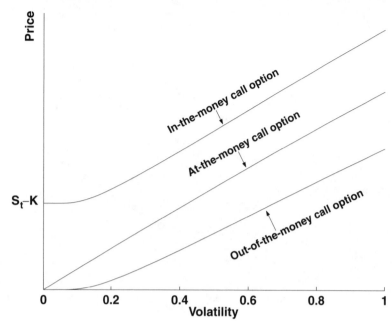

Figure 2.2 Variation of the price of a call option with volatility.

the higher the option price. This has to do with the fact that losses are bounded from below by the option price, but profits can be unlimited. Figures 2.2 and 2.3 show the variation of the option price with volatility for the call and the put option, respectively. Note the similarity between variations of the call and put option prices with volatility.

- *Dividends.* Consider an option on the stock Unilever with a strike price of $50 and the expiration date is in 1 year. Again, the stock price is $50. If in 6 months a dividend of $1 per stock is to be paid, this will cause the stock price to drop by $1. For that reason this dividend is favourable for a put option on Unilever and unfavourable for a call option on Unilever. In general,

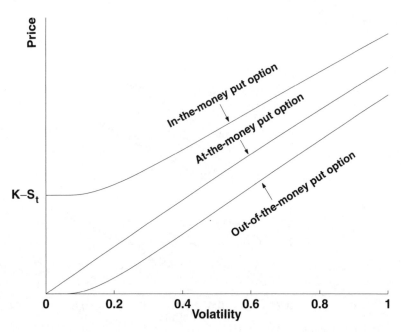

Figure 2.3   Variation of the price of a put option with volatility.

dividends will cause reductions in call option prices and the prices of put options to increase.

Now that it is clear which variables the price of an option should depend on, it is time to state the Black–Scholes formula. The Black–Scholes formula gives the price of an option in terms of its characteristics. It is beyond the scope of this book to actually prove this formula. Although it looks very complicated, do not be deterred. It is only for the sake of completeness that the Black–Scholes is stated here. It is perfectly possible to work with options without fully understanding the Black–Scholes formula. The most important thing to remember from the Black–Scholes formula is that it depends on the strike price (K), stock price (S_t), time to maturity $(T - t)$, interest rate (r), volatility (σ) and dividends. Because dividends make the theory unnecessarily complicated, this book will only deal with non-dividend paying stocks. In this case dividends can be left out. The Black–Scholes formula uses the following notation:

c_t = Price of a European call option at time t;

p_t = Price of a European put option at time t;

S_t = Price of the underlying stock at time t;

$T - t$ = Time to maturity;

K = Strike price of the option;

σ = Volatility of the underlying stock;

r = Interest rate.

The prices, at time t, of a European call option c_t and a European put option p_t are given by:

$$c_t = S_t N(d_1) - K e^{-r(T-t)} N(d_2), \qquad (2.1)$$

$$p_t = K e^{-r(T-t)} N(-d_2) - S_t N(-d_1) \qquad (2.2)$$

In these formulae, $N(x)$ is the standard Normal distribution, and d_1, d_2 are defined as:

$$d_1 = \frac{\ln\left(\dfrac{S_t}{K}\right) + \left(r + \frac{1}{2}\sigma^2\right)(T - t)}{\sigma\sqrt{T - t}} \qquad (2.3)$$

$$d_2 = d_1 - \sigma\sqrt{T - t} \qquad (2.4)$$

Of course, the above formulae reflect the fact that the price of an option on a non-dividend paying stock depends on the strike price, price of the underlying stock, time to maturity, volatility of the underlying stock and the interest rate. The next three subsections will elaborate on the Black–Scholes formula.

2.1   VOLATILITY AND THE BLACK–SCHOLES FORMULA

The volatility used in the Black–Scholes formula is actually more difficult than depicted before. In the Black–Scholes formula σ is the standard deviation of the natural logarithmic returns of the stock price, instead of just the standard deviation of the stock price. This means that if, over 3 days, a stock has a price trend of \$50, \$55, \$53, the volatility per day is the standard deviation of $\ln(55) - \ln(50) = \ln\left(\frac{55}{50}\right)$ and $\ln(53) - \ln(55) = \ln\left(\frac{53}{55}\right)$, rather than just the standard deviation of the percentage changes in stock price. Furthermore, it is important that the unit of time of volatility coincides with the unit of time of the time to maturity and with the unit of time of the interest rate. So, if the time to maturity and interest rate are expressed in years, volatility should also be expressed in years. Luckily, there is an easy formula to switch from volatility per (trading) day to volatility per annum (cf. p. 231 of Hull, 1993):

$$\begin{array}{c} \text{Volatility per} \\ \text{annum} \end{array} = \begin{array}{c} \text{Volatility per} \\ \text{trading day} \end{array} \times \sqrt{\begin{array}{c} \text{Number of trading} \\ \text{days per annum} \end{array}}$$

$$(2.5)$$

As mentioned earlier, the higher the volatility the higher the option price. This also becomes clear when looking at the Black–Scholes formula. The derivative of the option price with respect to the volatility gives the price's sensitivity to volatility. If this derivative is positive it means that the price increases as volatility increases. This is exactly what appears to be the case if the derivatives of formulae (2.1) and (2.2) are taken with respect to σ:

$$\nu_{\text{call,European}} = \frac{\partial c_t}{\partial \sigma} = \frac{1}{\sqrt{2\pi}} e^{-\frac{d_1^2}{2}} S_t \sqrt{T-t} > 0 \quad (2.6)$$

$$\nu_{\text{put,European}} = \frac{\partial p_t}{\partial \sigma} = \frac{1}{\sqrt{2\pi}} e^{-\frac{d_1^2}{2}} S_t \sqrt{T-t} > 0 \quad (2.7)$$

The option price's sensitivity to volatility is often referred to as *vega*, and is the same for both European call and put options. In this book 'vega' is indicated with the Greek letter ν.[1]

2.2 INTEREST RATE AND THE BLACK–SCHOLES FORMULA

In the previous section it was mentioned that it is important that r, σ and $T-t$ are expressed in the same unit of time. In the same section it was shown how to switch from volatility per annum to volatility per trading day. To switch from interest rate per annum to interest rate per trading day is very straightforward. The following relationship holds between interest rate per annum and interest rate per trading day.

---

[1] Vega is not actually a Greek letter, but in option theory it is still referred to as an option Greek.

$$\frac{\text{Interest rate}}{\text{per annum}} = \frac{\text{Interest rate per}}{\text{trading day}} \times \frac{\text{Number of trading}}{\text{days per annum}}$$

(2.8)

The same analysis as in Section 2.1 can be conducted for the interest rate. The derivative of the option price with respect to the interest rate gives its sensitivity to the interest rate. Of course, since the price of a European put option decreases as the interest rate increases, this derivative should be negative for the put option. For a call option it is hard to deduce economically what the sign of this derivative should be. The next formulae give for both the call and the put option the sign of the derivative of the option price with respect to the interest rate. It appears that for the call option this derivative is positive, which means that the price of the call option increases as the interest rate increases:

$$\rho_{\text{call,European}} = \frac{\partial c_t}{\partial r} = K(T - t) \, e^{-r(T-t)} N(d_2) > 0 \qquad (2.9)$$

$$\rho_{\text{put,European}} = \frac{\partial p_t}{\partial r} = -K(T - t) \, e^{-r(T-t)} N(-d_2) < 0 \quad (2.10)$$

From an economical point of view it is logical that the price of a European put option is less when the interest rate is higher. Because both the fact that expected growth rates on stocks increase as well as the fact that higher interest rates are earned on savings accounts cause the price to decrease. Since, for a European call option, the first effect causes the price to increase and the second to decrease, it is less obvious what happens to the price. Formula (2.9) states that the price of a European call option increases if the interest rate increases. This means that the first effect more than offsets the second. Because, for a put option, there are two effects causing the price to decrease, a put option is more sensitive to interest rate changes than a call option, which has one effect causing the price to decrease and one effect causing it to increase. The option price's sensitivity to the interest rate is often referred to as *rho*, and is indicated with the Greek letter ρ.

2.3 PRICING AMERICAN OPTIONS

The Black–Scholes formula is one way of deriving the fair price of an option. This works well for European options, but for American put options and American call options on dividend paying stocks this method does not work any longer. For that reason there is another model, the binomial tree model. In practice, the binomial tree model is a popular tool for determining the price of American options. The binomial tree model reaches a price by simulating price trends and looking at different points in time, whether it is optimal to exercise the option or not. This is different from the Black–Scholes model, but it still uses the same variables. For that reason, to get an understanding of options it is enough or maybe better to use the Black–Scholes model.

Chapter
3

....

DIVIDENDS AND THEIR EFFECT ON OPTIONS

Although dividends are not the first concern of an option trader it is important to understand how they affect option pricing. In this section this will be explained and the reader will be introduced to *forwards*.

3.1 FORWARDS

Forwards are agreements to buy or sell shares at a future point in time without having to make a payment up front. Unlike an option, the buyer of a forward does not have an option at expiry. For example, the buyer of a 6-month forward in Royal Dutch/Shell commits himself to buying shares in Royal Dutch/Shell at a pre-agreed price determined by the forward contract. The natural question is, of course: What should this pre-agreed price be? Just like Black and Scholes did for the pricing of an option the price is determined by how much it will cost to hedge the forward position. To show this, consider the following example. An investment bank sells a 2-year forward on Royal Dutch/Shell to an investor. Suppose that the stock is trading at $40, the interest rate is 5% per year and after 1 year Royal Dutch/Shell will pay a dividend of $1. Because the bank sells the forward it commits itself to selling a Royal Dutch/Shell share in 2 years' time. The bank will hedge itself by buying a Royal Dutch/Shell share today. By buying a Royal Dutch/Shell share the bank pays $40, over which it will pay interest for the next 2 years. However, since the bank is long a Royal Dutch/Shell share it will receive a dividend of $1 in 1 year's time. So, over the first year the bank will pay interest on \$40 and over the second year interest on \$39. This means the price of the forward should be:

$$F = 40 + 40 \times 0.05 + 39 \times 0.05 - 1 = 42.95 \quad (3.1)$$

A more general formula for the forward price is:

$$F = \text{Price of underlying} + \text{Cost of carry} \quad (3.2)$$

In the previous example the cost of carry is the interest the bank has to pay to hold the stock minus the dividend it receives for holding the stock.

3.2 PRICING OF STOCK OPTIONS INCLUDING DIVIDENDS

When dividends are known to be paid at specific points in time it is easy to adjust the Black–Scholes formula such that it gives the right option price. The only change one needs to make is to adjust the stock price. The reason for this is that a dividend payment will cause the stock price to go down by exactly the amount of the dividend. So, in order to get the right option price one needs to subtract the present value of the dividends paid during the term of the option from the current stock price, which can then be plugged into the Black–Scholes formula – see equations (2.1) and (2.2). As an example, consider a 1-year call option on Daimler Chrysler (DCX) with a strike price of \$40. Suppose DCX is currently trading at \$40, the interest rate is 5%, stock price volatility is 20% per annum and there are two dividends in the next year, one of \$1 after 2 months and another of \$0.5 after 8 months. It is now possible to calculate the present value of the dividends and subtract it from the current stock level. For the present value calculation see Section 3.3:

$$\text{PV of dividends} = e^{\{-\frac{2}{12}\times 0.05\}} \times 1 + e^{\{-\frac{8}{12}\times 0.05\}} \times 0.5$$

$$= 1.4753 \tag{3.3}$$

Now the option price can be calculated by plugging into the Black–Scholes formula – see equation (2.1) – a stock price of $S_t = 40 - 1.4753 = 38.5247$ and using $K = 40$, $r = 0.05$, $\sigma = 0.2$ and $T - t = 1$:

$$d_1 = \frac{\ln\left(\frac{38.527}{40}\right) + \left(0.05 + \frac{1}{2}\times 0.2^2\right)\times 1}{0.2 \times \sqrt{1}} = 0.1621 \tag{3.4}$$

$$d_2 = d_1 - 0.2 \times \sqrt{1} = -0.0379 \tag{3.5}$$

So, the price of the call option will be:

$$c_t = 38.5247 \times N(0.1621) - 40 \times e^{-0.05}N(-0.0379)$$

$$= 3.2934 \tag{3.6}$$

3.3 PRICING OPTIONS IN TERMS OF THE FORWARD

Instead of expressing the option price in terms of the current stock price, interest rate and expected dividends it makes it more intuitive to price an option in terms of the forward, which comprises all these three components. The easiest way to rewrite the Black–Scholes formula in terms of the forward is to assume a dividend yield rather than dividends paid out at discrete points in time. This means that a continuous dividend payout is assumed. Although this is not what happens in practice one can calculate the dividend yield in such a way that the present value of the dividend payments is equal to $S_t(1 - e^{-d(T-t)})$, where d is the dividend yield. So, if the dividend yield is assumed to be d and the interest rate is r the forward at time t can be expressed as:

$$F_t = S_t \times e^{\{r(T-t)\}} \times e^{\{-d(T-t)\}}$$

$$= S_t \times e^{\{(r-d)(T-t)\}} \qquad (3.7)$$

From the above equation it is clear that dividends lower the price of the forward and interest rates increase it. As shown in the previous subsection one can calculate the price of an option by putting a stock price equal to $S_t \times e^{\{-d(T-t)\}}$ into the Black–Scholes formula. By doing this one can easily rearrange the Black–Scholes formula to express the price of an option in terms of the forward. The price of the call will then be expressed as:

$$c_t = S_t\, e^{-d(T-t)} N(d_1) - K\, e^{-r(T-t)} N(d_2)$$

$$= e^{-r(T-t)} F_t N(d_1) - K\, e^{-r(T-t)} N(d_2) \qquad (3.8)$$

In the same way the price of the put can be expressed as:

$$p_t = K\, e^{-r(T-t)} N(-d_2) - e^{-r(T-t)} F_t N(-d_1) \qquad (3.9)$$

where d_1 and d_2 look like:

$$d_1 = \frac{\ln\left(\frac{S_t e^{-d(T-t)}}{K}\right) + \left(r + \frac{1}{2}\sigma^2\right)(T-t)}{\sigma\sqrt{T-t}}$$

$$= \frac{\ln\left(\frac{e^{-r(T-t)}F_t}{K}\right) + \left(\frac{1}{2}\sigma^2\right)(T-t)}{\sigma\sqrt{T-t}} \tag{3.10}$$

$$d_2 = d_1 - \sigma\sqrt{T-t} \tag{3.11}$$

3.4 DIVIDEND RISK FOR OPTIONS

The problem option traders face when trading options is that they usually do not know the exact dividends a company is due to pay out. So, the only way to price an option is to estimate the future dividends a company is expected to pay. Usually, it is relatively easy to estimate the dividends for the near future; however, the further one goes into the future the harder it gets. This is because dividends are very much related to the profitability of a company. In this perspective it is also useful to think of an option price in terms of the forward. If the actual dividends a company has paid out are higher than the trader had expected, the trader's forward should have been lower which causes the prices of call options to go down because it is less likely that the call option will expire in the money. With the same argument the prices of put options will go up because they are more likely to expire in the money. So, the risk an option trader faces when buying a call option is that the dividends appear to be higher than he had expected, and when buying a put option that they appear to be lower than he had expected. Of course, the reverse holds for selling either a call or a put. When it comes to assessing the risks of dividends it is best to think of the option price in terms of the forward. If the dividends go up the forward will go down which makes it less likely that a call option will expire in the money, so the price will go down. A put will more likely expire in the money, so the price will go up. If dividends go down the forward will go up, so the price of a call goes up and the price of a put goes down. In conclusion, to assess how dividend or interest rate changes affect the price of an option just think about what happens to the forward. If the forward goes down put options get more expensive and calls less expensive. If the forward goes up call options get more expensive and put options less expensive.

3.5 SYNTHETICS

It is possible to synthetically create a forward by buying a call option and selling a put option with the forward price as the strike. Intuitively, this can easily be seen by adding up the respective payoff graphs as done in Figure 3.1. This figure also shows that a synthetic has the same dynamics as a normal share, which is what one would expect. Since forwards do not cost anything it should also be the case that a call minus a put with the forward price as the strike is worth 0. Bringing the put–call parity from Section 3.6

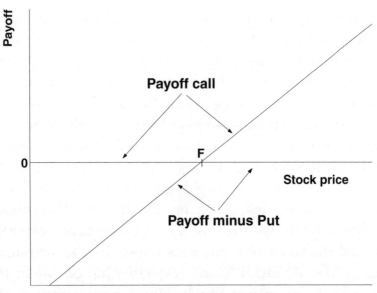

Figure 3.1 Synthetic payoff.

back into memory will make this clear. The put–call parity for non-dividend paying stocks states:

$$c_t - p_t = S_t - Ke^{-r(T-t)} \qquad (3.12)$$

The forward of a non-dividend paying stock is $F = S_t\, e^{r(T-t)}$, which shows that if the strike price for both the call and the put is the forward price the call minus the put, the synthetic, is worth 0. In the same way this can be proved for options on dividend paying stocks. However, in this case the put–call parity is:

$$c_t - p_t = S_t - K\, e^{-(r-d)(T-t)} \qquad (3.13)$$

where d is the dividend yield. In practice, one would only see synthetic forwards on specific strikes, not necessarily on the forward price.

Chapter
4

. . . .

IMPLIED VOLATILITY

Although implied volatility is a relatively easy concept it is usually thought to be complicated. This is because things can get confusing. Implied volatility is not just a theoretical concept, it also depends on the simple market phenomenon of supply and demand. Before implied volatility is explained in more detail, volatility will be elaborated on.

As mentioned earlier volatility is a measure for the movement of the stock price. To be precise, it is the standard deviation of the natural logarithm of the returns of the stock price. Although this is the official definition, it is more important to understand which time period this volatility relates to in the Black–Scholes formula. The answer is of course simple, it is the volatility of the stock price during the term of the option. It is simple, but it is good to be aware of this fact, since this implies that whenever an investor wants to buy an option he does not know what the volatility will be during the term of the option. This, in turn, makes it impossible for him to calculate the fair price of the option. However, he can try to estimate this volatility by looking at what the volatility has been so far, the historic volatility. Although there are techniques to estimate the volatility accurately, he will never be able to say with certainty what the volatility will be during the term of the option. In fact, from all the variables the Black–Scholes formula uses to determine the price of an option on a non-dividend paying stock, volatility is the only one that is really open to interpretation. This is obvious for the stock price, strike price and time to maturity, but for the interest rate this is less obvious. Because, for the same reason volatility is not known, one would argue that an investor does not know what the interest rate will be during the term of the option. However, it is possible to estimate the interest rate so accurately that this variable can effectively be treated as known. With this knowledge it is easy to explain the concept of implied volatility.

The price of an option comes about from supply and demand. This is of course confusing. The Black–Scholes formula gives the price of an option, which would suggest there could only be one price for an option, regardless of supply and demand. But, as has been pointed out, at the time an investor has to decide whether or not to buy an option, he does not know what the volatility of the option will be during the term of this option. So, different market participants have different views on what the volatility will be, and therefore have different views on what should be the fair price of an option. Now an interesting situation arises. There is the Black–Scholes formula which gives the price of an option on a non-dividend paying stock in terms of the stock price, strike price, time to maturity, interest rate and volatility, but at the same time the price of this option is set by supply and demand. If an investor wants to know whether he should buy a specific option he could estimate what he thinks the volatility should be and use this volatility to plug into the Black–Scholes formula in order to calculate the price he is prepared to pay for this option. Or he could determine which volatility gives the option price set by the market and compare it with what he thinks is the right volatility. This can be done by equating the Black–Scholes formula with the market price of the option, which is an equation in one unknown, namely the volatility. An equation in one unknown can always be solved[1] and the volatility obtained in this way is called the 'implied volatility'. This is a logical name because, in calculating it, the market price of an option is used. Which means that the calculated volatility is implied by the market and, therefore, it tells what the market thinks the volatility of the underlying stock will be during the term of the option. **In conclusion, the implied volatility is nothing more than that volatility, such that when it is substituted into the Black–Scholes formula the output is equal to the market price of the option.** The idea of implied volatility is illustrated by the following example, which is based on the example on p. 229 of Hull (1993).

4.1 EXAMPLE[2]

Suppose that the value of a European call option on a non-dividend paying stock is $3.67 when $S_t = 33$, $K = 30$, $r = 0.05$ and $T - t = 0.25$ (In this example $T - t$ is expressed in years, so $T - t = 0.25$ is a time to maturity of 3 months.) The implied volatility is that value of σ which, when substituted into formula (2.1) together with $S_t = 33$, $K = 30$, $r = 0.05$ and $T - t = 0.25$, gives $c_t = 3.67$. Although this is really only an equation in one unknown,

---

[1] Because the Black–Scholes formula contains the Normal distribution, this particular equation in the unknown σ cannot be solved analytically. However, there are methods, like the Newton–Raphson method, to solve it to any required accuracy. An example of such a method will be treated shortly.

[2] This example is almost identical to the example on p. 229 of Hull (1993), only the numbers are different.

it cannot be reduced to an expression in which σ is expressed as a function of S_t, K, r, $T - t$ and c_t. However, an iterative search procedure can be used to find the implied σ. To start with, the value $\sigma = 0.15$ could be used. This gives a value of c_t equal to 3.4518, which is too low. Since c_t is an increasing function of σ, a higher value of σ is required. Next, a value of $\sigma = 0.25$ could be tried. This gives a value of c_t equal to 3.7925, which is too high and means that σ lies between 0.15 and 0.25. Next, a value of 0.20 can be tried for σ. This will prove to be too low, deriving that σ lies between 0.20 and 0.25. Proceeding in this way the range for σ can be halved at each iteration and the correct value of σ can be calculated to any required accuracy. In this example, the implied volatility is 0.22 or 22% per annum. Note that because $T - t$ was expressed in years, the implied volatility is also expressed in years.

4.2   STRATEGY AND IMPLIED VOLATILITY

Consider an option trader who wants to decide upon the implied volatility if he bought the option in the previous example or not. As was shown in this example, the implied volatility of this option is 22% per annum. Suppose also that he thinks that the underlying stock will have a volatility of 1.5% per trading day during the term of the option. Now he can use formula (2.5) to determine if he should buy the option. If there are 256 trading days in each year, this would mean that he thinks that the volatility per annum is $1.5 \times \sqrt{256} = 24\%$. As stated before, the higher the volatility the higher the price of the option. Because the option trader thinks the volatility should be 24% per annum and the market thinks it will be 22%, it means that the option trader thinks that the option is worth more than he has to pay for it on the market. In this case, the option trader should buy the option. But, if he thinks the volatility will be 1% per trading day he should not buy the option. Because 1% per trading day means a volatility of $1 \times \sqrt{256} = 16\%$ per annum, and this would imply that he thinks the option is worth less than he has to pay for it on the market. **In general, if an investor thinks the implied volatility of an option is too high he should not buy the option, whereas if he thinks it is too low he should buy the option**. In this analysis it is important that volatilities are compared over the same period of time. So, a volatility per trading day can only be compared with another volatiltity if this one is also expressed in trading days, and of course the same holds for volatilities expressed in years or any other unit of time.

Chapter

5

....

DELTA

Delta measures the sensitivity of the option price to the stock price while all other variables remain unchanged. Mathematically, it is the derivative of the option price with respect to the stock price. So, if the delta of an option is 0.5, it means that – if the stock price increases by \$1 – the option price increases by \$0.5,[1] and if the stock price decreases by a small amount the option price decreases by 50% of that amount. If delta is negative the reverse holds. Suppose an option has a delta of −0.5. In this case, if the stock price increases by \$1 the option price decreases by \$0.5, and if the stock price decreases by \$1 the option price increases by \$0.5. The delta of a put option is negative, since the price of a put option decreases as the stock price increases. For a call option the reverse holds, since the price of a call option increases as the stock price increases. **The delta of a call option is between 0 and 1, and for a put option it is between −1 and 0.** It was argued that the delta of a call option had to be greater than 0. But why does the delta of a call option have to be less than 1? To answer this question it is important to know what comprises the price of a call option. This price has an *intrinsic*[2] part and an *option* part. It has an *intrinsic* part since the price of a call option on a non-dividend paying[3] stock is always at least as much as the intrinsic value. After all, an American call option can be

---

[1] This is not totally correct because if the stock price changes, δ also changes. So, in fact, it should be that if the stock price changes by a small amount the option price changes by 50% of that amount. But, for the sake of this example it is expressed in a \$1 stock price movement.

[2] The intrinsic value of an option is the payoff of that option were it exercised immediately. See Section 1.3.

[3] The value of a European call option on a dividend paying stock can be less than intrinsic, which will be shown in Section 5.3.

exercised immediately to get a payoff equal to the intrinsic value of the option, and, for the European call option, the strategy[4] of going long the call option and shorting the underlying stock locks in a discounted payoff greater than the intrinsic value. There is also an *option* part to the price of the option, since payoffs can be unlimited but are bounded from below by 0 (an investor can choose not to do anything). This means that the investor's discounted expected payoff is always higher than the intrinsic value. Logically, the *option* part is defined as the discounted expected payoff of the option minus the intrinsic value. In conclusion, an investor who owns a call option can guarantee himself a payoff equal to the intrinsic value by exercising immediately, and if he chooses not to exercise the option immediately his discounted expected payoff is higher than the intrinsic value. Now, it is easy to see why the delta of a call option has to be less than 1. To show this, it is convenient to distinguish between an *in-the-money* and an *out-of-the-money* call option, respectively. Suppose the delta of an *in-the-money* call option is bigger than 1. This would mean that if the stock price increased by $1, the option price would increase by more than $1. Since a $1 increase in stock price implies a $1 increase in intrinsic value of the call option, this implies that the *option* part of the price also increases. But this cannot be true. Since, if the stock price has increased by $1, it is less likely that the stock price will drop below the strike price and for that reason the downside risk being bounded[5] becomes less valuable,

---

[4] Argument put forward on p. 158 of Hull (1993).
[5] See Section 1.3.

which in turn implies that the *option* part becomes less valuable. The same conclusion can be drawn if the stock price decreased by $1. So, if the delta of an *in-the-money* call option were bigger than 1, a $1 decrease in stock price would cause the option price to decrease by more than the intrinsic value, implying that the *option* part of the price becomes less. But, in this case this is a contradiction, because the downside risk being bounded becomes more valuable. This shows that the delta of an *in-the-money* call option cannot be bigger than 1, so it has to be less than 1. In the same way, it can be argued that the delta of an *in-the-money* put[6] option has to lie between -1 and 0. For an *out-of-the-money* call or put option it is even more straightforward. Because, in this case, the intrinsic value of the option is 0, the price only consists of the *option* part. Recalling that the *option* part is defined as the discounted expected payoff minus the intrinsic value, this means that the price is equal to the discounted expected payoff. Since the change in discounted expected payoff of an *out-of-the-money* option is less than the change in stock price (otherwise, the probability that this change in payoff is realized would be 1, which is clearly not true), it is easy to see that the delta of an *out-of-the-money* call option lies between 0 and 1 and the delta of an *out-of-the-money* put option lies between -1 and 0. These phenomena also become clear if the derivatives of formulae (2.1) and (2.2) are taken with respect to the stock price, S_t. The

---

[6] One could think that the European put option case differs slightly, since the price of this option is not necessarily as much as the intrinsic value. But, by noting that in this case the *option* part is negative and since the *intrinsic* part can never change by more than the change in stock price, the same reasoning still holds.

next two formulae are the deltas of the European call and European put option on a non-dividend paying stock, respectively:

$$\delta_{\text{call,European}} = \frac{\partial c_t}{\partial S_t} = N(d_1) > 0 \qquad (5.1)$$

$$\delta_{\text{put,European}} = \frac{\partial p_t}{\partial S_t} = -N(-d_1) < 0 \qquad (5.2)$$

Formulae (5.1) and (5.2) not only point out that the δ of a European call option is positive and the δ of a European put option is negative, they also show that the δ of a European call option lies between 0 and 1 and of a European put between -1 and 0. This last mentioned observation stems from the fact that $N(d_1)$ and $N(-d_1)$ lie between 0 and 1. An interesting question is, of course: When is the δ of a call option 0 and when is it 1? Again, by dividing the option price into an *intrinsic* part and an *option* part the answer to this question is easily given. Consider a call option which is far in the money, which means that the stock price is substantially higher than the strike price of the call option. For this option, the fact that the downside risk is bounded from below is virtually not worth anything. So, the price of this call option is equal to the intrinsic value. This implies that if the stock price goes up by \$1 the option price also has to go up by \$1, since otherwise the option price will be less than the intrinsic value. For the same reason, if the stock price goes down by \$1 the option price also goes down by \$1. This shows that the δ of a far *in-the-money* call option is 1. Now consider a far *out-of-the-money* call option, which means that the stock price is substantially less

Table 5.1   Extreme delta values.

Type of option	Delta (δ)
Far in-the-money call option	1
Far out-of-the-money call option	0
Far in-the-money put option	-1
Far out-of-the-money put option	0

than the strike price of the option. This option is not worth anything, since the probability that a profit will be made is 0. Whether the price of the stock goes up or down the call option will still not be worth anything. This shows that a far *out-of-the-money* call option has a δ of 0. With a similar reasoning one would find that a far *in-the-money* put option (stock price is substantially less than the strike price of the option) has a δ of -1 and the δ of a far *out-of-the-money* put option (stock price is substantially higher than the strike price of the option) is 0. Table 5.1 summarizes these observations, and Figures 5.1 and 5.2 show the variation of delta with the stock price for the call and the put option, respectively.

5.1   DELTA-HEDGING

'Hedging' literally means reducing the risk. So, if an investor has a portfolio which exposes him to a high risk, he could try to hedge this portfolio in order to reduce his risk. The question arises: How can a holder of a stock option hedge himself against future stock movements? This question is easily answered with the knowledge of delta. Consider an investor with 100 call options and each

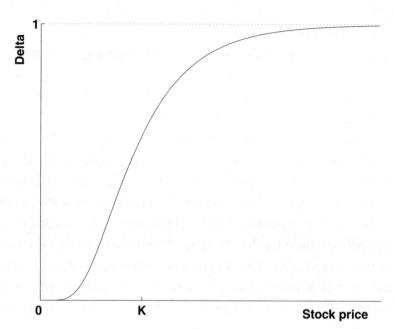

Figure 5.1 Variation of delta with stock price for a call option.

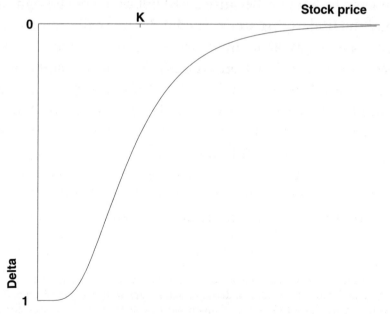

Figure 5.2 Variation of delta with stock price for a put option.

option has a delta of 0.5. This investor can hedge himself against future stock movements by **shorting** (selling) 50 of the underlying stocks. After all, if the stock price goes down by $1, the call option price decreases by $0.5, causing a loss of $50 (100 options times $-$0.5), but at the same time the investor makes a profit of $50[7] on the 50 stocks he had shorted. With this hedging method the investor not only makes no more losses, he also no longer makes any profits. Because, if the stock price goes up by $1, he makes a profit of $50 (100 options times $0.5) on the call option, but this is offset by the loss on the shorted underlying stocks. The same holds for a put option, but in this case the investor has to **buy** $|\delta|$[8] times the number of options of the underlying stock. It is logical that, in the case of a long call option, stocks have to be sold to hedge the position and, in the case of a long put option, stocks have to be bought. Because a call option gives the right to buy the underlying stock, the holder of a call option does not face a payoff at maturity if he is one stock short whenever the call option expires *in the money*, and whenever the call option expires *out of the money* if he does not hold a position in the underlying stock at all. Since, for call options very close to maturity, the probability that a call option will expire in the money is approximately equal to δ, this particular long call option is hedged if δ stocks are shorted. Although the probability that a call option with a longer time to maturity will expire in

---

[7] For each stock he received $1 more than he has to pay for it now.
[8] This is the absolute value of delta, which means that if $\delta = -0.5$, $|\delta| = 0.5$. Note that the absolute value is taken because the delta of a put option is negative.

the money is not equal to δ,[9] such a long call option is still hedged by shorting δ underlying stocks. This phenomenon will be explained in Section 7.5. Because a put option gives the right to sell the underlying stock, the holder of a put option does not face a payoff at maturity if he is one stock long whenever the put option expires *in the money*, and if the put option expires *out of the money* if he does not hold a position in the underlying stock at all. Since, for put options very close to expiration, the probability that a put option will expire in the money is approximately equal to $|\delta|$, this particular long put option is hedged if $|\delta|$ stocks are bought. Just like call options, for put options with longer times to maturity the probability that a put option expires in the money is not equal to $|\delta|$,[10] but such a put option is still hedged by buying $|\delta|$ underlying stocks. Another way to look at the difference between hedging a call option and a put option is by means of the sign of δ. The sign of the δ of a call option is positive and of a put option negative. So, to hedge either a long put option as well as a long call option, δ underlying stocks have to be shorted. But, since the δ of a put option is negative this hedging strategy effectively means that the underlying stocks have to be bought.

Black and Scholes showed that if **at any point in time** a long option is hedged by shorting the δ of the underlying

---

[9] The probability that a call option expires in the money is equal to $N(d_2)$ (cf. Appendix A). This explains why, for call options close to maturity, this probability is equal to δ.

[10] The probability that a put option expires in the money is equal to $N(-d_2)$ (cf. Appendix A). This explains why, for put options close to maturity, this probability is equal to $|\delta|$.

stocks, this portfolio is riskless, which means that the return on the portfolio is equal to the interest rate. Mathematically, the following portfolio is riskless (return on the portfolio is equal to the interest rate)

$$+1 : \quad \text{Option}$$
$$-\delta : \quad \text{Underlying stock.}$$

This means that if money is to be borrowed to set up this portfolio, the return on the portfolio is the interest rate and the borrowed money can be repaid with interest, making neither loss nor a profit. If money is to be received to set up this portfolio, the return on the portfolio is negative the interest rate, which cancels out the return on the money received for setting up the portfolio. Important in the analysis of Black and Scholes is the bold-face part, **at any point in time, since δ already changes if the stock price changes by a small amount and also with the passage of time.** This means, to really set up a riskless portfolio, the number of shorted stocks has to be adjusted continuously. Aside from the fact that this portfolio is only riskless if no transaction costs have to be paid for adjusting the number of stocks in the portfolio, this is physically impossible. In practice, the number of stocks in the portfolio is only adjusted according to the value of δ at discrete points in time. Such a hedging scheme is referred to as 'dynamic hedging', and whenever the number of shorted stocks is adjusted according to δ, this is referred to as making the portfolio *delta neutral*. Although, at this point, it may seem inconvenient that in practice it is only possible to hedge dynamically, it will become apparent that this is exactly why option traders make a profit.

5.2 THE MOST DIVIDEND-SENSITIVE OPTIONS

Since there is always a chance that a company will change its dividend payments it is good to have a feel for which options are most dividend-sensitive. In Section 3.2 it was shown that the price of an option on a dividend paying stock can easily be calculated by putting into the Black–Scholes formula a stock price S_t equal to the current stock price minus the present value of the dividends. The delta measures the sensitivity of an option price to a change in the underlying S_t. From this it is clear that an option with a large delta in absolute terms will be very sensitive to dividend changes. This means that far in-the-money options as well as synthetics have large dividend exposures.

5.3 EXERCISE-READY AMERICAN CALLS ON DIVIDEND PAYING STOCKS

Section 1.4 showed that it is never optimal to exercise early a call option on a non-dividend paying stock and as a result prices of American and European call options are the same for non-dividend paying stocks. However, it can be optimal to exercise early an American call option on a dividend paying stock. For that reason the price of an

American call option on a dividend paying stock can differ from its European counterpart. To see this consider an American call option on the French pharmaceutical company Sanofi-Aventis with a strike price of $50 and a maturity of 3 months. Sanofi is currently trading at $80 and the stock is due to go ex-dividend[11] tomorrow with a payable dividend of $1.50. Since this option is clearly far in the money the *time value*[12] of this option is very little, which means that this option has a very high delta. Since the stock will go ex-dividend tomorrow one can expect the share price to drop by $1.50 and as a result the in-trinsic value of the option to go from $30 to $28.50. The only way the option can regain this drop in intrinsic value is by a sharp increase in time value. However, the option is so far in the money that, although the time value will increase slightly, it will never be enough to make up for the loss in intrinsic value. Assuming that the time value of this option goes from $0.02 to $0.10 with the stock dropping to $78.50, the option on the ex-dividend date is worth $28.60 where the day before it was worth $30.02. From the above it is clear that it is optimal to exercise the $50.00 call on Sanofi. When comparing the price of the European counterpart of the above option the day before the stock goes ex-dividend, one would expect this price to be equal to the price of the American option on the ex-

---

[11] A stock trading ex-dividend means that whoever purchases this stock is no longer entitled to receive the dividend. As a result the stock will theoret-ically be worth less by exactly the amount of the dividend payable. If it takes 2 days to settle the shares of a company, the company will trade ex-dividend 2 days before the record date of the dividend.

[12] The time value of an option is equal to the *option* part, as described in Chapter 5.

dividend date plus the time value of the option of the day before – that is, $28.62.

When determining whether an American call option on a dividend paying stock is exercisable, one has to realize first that one would only exercise an American call option the day before the stock goes ex-dividend. Because, even if the American call option is a clear exercise, there is always a chance that the stock will drop considerably giving the option a large time value again, and because the option was delta-hedged, one would have made the same amount of money on stocks that were shorted as on the drop in intrinsic value (delta needs to have been very close to 1 otherwise it can never be an exercise). Bearing this in mind there are basically three option character-istics that signal that an American call option on a divi-dend paying stock is an exercise. The first one is that the delta of the option should be very close to 1, which means that the time value is very little. Second, the American option should be worth almost intrinsic the day before the stock goes ex-dividend. This second characteristic is in fact the most reliable one because it is basically telling one that exercising the option will not be costly. Third, the European call option should be worth less than in-trinsic the day before the stock goes ex-dividend and, therefore, be less than the American call. However, just comparing the European with the American call can be tricky because, when there are several dividend pay-ments during the term of the option, the European call will almost always be worth less.

Although the aforementioned three characteristics give good guidelines as to whether an American call on a dividend paying stock is exercisable, the only way to be sure is by testing the following. If on the day before the stock goes ex-dividend the price of an American call is worth more than the same American call, only then – with the dividend taken out and a share price which is the current share price less the dividend – should the call be exercised.[13] If this is not the case the call should not be exercised.

---

[13] Obviously, there is a 1-day difference. So, the American call should really be compared with the same American call and only then, with the dividend taken out and a share price equal to the current share price less the dividend, should the start date of the call be moved 1 day forward.

Chapter
6

....

THREE OTHER GREEKS

In this chapter three other Greeks will be introduced – respectively, gamma, theta and vega. Gamma measures delta's sensitivity to the stock price, theta measures the option price's sensitivity to the passage of time, and vega measures the option price's sensitivity to volatility.

6.1 GAMMA

Previously, in most examples concerning δ it was said that a \$1 change in stock price would cause the option price to change by δ. Although in these examples this is a useful interpretation of δ, it is not totally correct. This is because δ changes even if the stock price changes by a small amount and also with the passage of time. Thus, while the stock price changes by \$1, δ takes many different values. This means that it is not correct to calculate the option price change, caused by a \$1 change in stock price, using only one δ-value. The right way to deal with δ is, if the stock price changes by a small[1] amount, then the option price changes by δ times this amount. Since δ changes if the stock price changes, it would be nice to have a unit that measures delta's sensitivity to stock price movements. This unit is called 'gamma' and is indicated by the Greek letter γ. Mathematically, γ is the derivative of δ with respect to the stock price. If gamma is small, stock price movements only cause small changes in delta. However, if gamma is large, delta is highly sensitive to stock price changes. So, an investor who owns an option with a large gamma has to adjust the number of stocks in

---

[1] Here 'small' means really small. Even \$0.01 is too much.

his portfolio frequently to keep this portfolio delta-neutral. Both call and put options have a positive gamma and, as will be shown shortly, these gammas appear to be the same for both European call and put options. The fact that gamma is positive for both the call and the put option is logical. After all, the delta of a call option is an increasing function in the stock price, and increases from 0 to 1 as the stock price increases from 0 to infinity; the delta of a put option increases from -1 to 0 as the stock price increases from 0 to infinity. Before the formula of gamma is given for the European call and put option, note that gamma is the second derivative of the option price with respect to the stock price. Indeed, delta is the first derivative of the option price with respect to the stock price, and because gamma is the derivative of delta with respect to the stock price it is clear that this is true. For a European call and put option, gamma is given by:

$$\gamma_{\text{call,European}} = \frac{\partial \delta}{\partial S_t} = \frac{\partial^2 c_t}{\partial (S_t)^2} = \frac{N'(d_1)}{S_t \sigma \sqrt{T-t}} > 0 \quad (6.1)$$

$$\gamma_{\text{put,European}} = \frac{\partial \delta}{\partial S_t} = \frac{\partial^2 c_t}{\partial (S_t)^2} = \frac{N'(d_1)}{S_t \sigma \sqrt{T-t}} > 0 \quad (6.2)$$

where d_1 is defined as in equation (2.3) and:

$$N'(x) = 1\sqrt{2\pi}\, e^{-x^2 2} \quad (6.3)$$

The above formulae again show that the gamma of a European call option is equal to the gamma of a European put option. Respectively, Figures 6.1 and 6.2 indicate the way in which gamma varies with the stock price and the time to maturity.

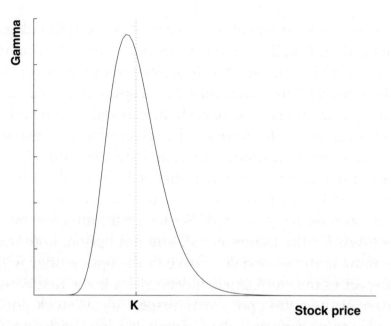

Figure 6.1   Variation of gamma with stock price.

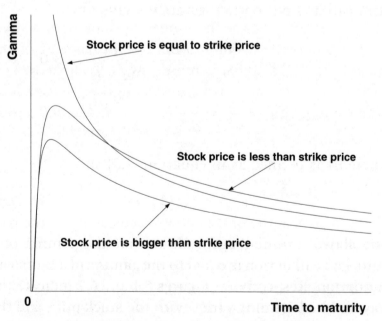

Figure 6.2   Variation of gamma with time to maturity.

It is worth noting that gamma becomes very big if an at-the-money option is close to expiring. This is caused by the fact that small stock price changes heavily affect the probability that this option will expire in the money. Since, for options close to expiration, $|\delta|$ is approximately equal to this probability, small stock price changes heavily affect δ. This explains why at-the-money options close to maturity have big gammas.

Lastly, from a practical point of a view it is good to remember that the gamma of any option is largest when it is close to 'at the money'. This has the direct implication that prices of options close to 'at the money' are very sensitive to stock price movements and, therefore, need to be re-hedged frequently. Also, when the stock is close to the strike, options with a short time to maturity have higher gammas than options with a long time to maturity. So, the prices of at-the-money options with a short time to maturity are more sensitive to changes in the underlying stock and, therefore, need to be re-hedged more frequently than at-the-money options with a long time to maturity.

6.2 THETA

Theta measures the option price's sensitivity to the passage of time while all other variables remain unchanged. So, it is the rate of change of the option price with respect to time, and is usually indicated by the Greek letter θ. It is good to be aware of the impact of theta. Even if variables like stock price, interest rate and volatility remain

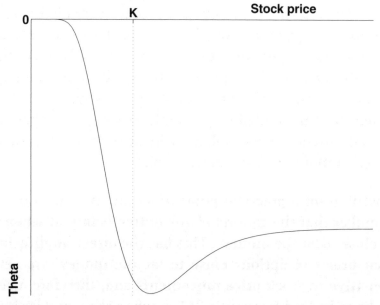

Figure 6.3 Variation of theta with stock price for a European call option, when the interest rate is strictly positive.

unchanged, the option price will still change. Mathematically, theta is the derivative of the option price with respect to time. The theta of a European call option is always negative, which means that as time passes the option price will decrease. The variation of theta with stock price for a European call option is plotted in Figure 6.3. The variation of theta with time to maturity for a European call option is plotted in Figure 6.4. The theta of a European put option is almost always negative. An example of a European put option with a positive theta could be an in-the-money European put option on a non-dividend paying stock, provided the interest rate is strictly positive. For a far in-the-money put option this can be seen intuitively. After all, the fact that the upward risk is bounded is not worth anything for a far in-the-

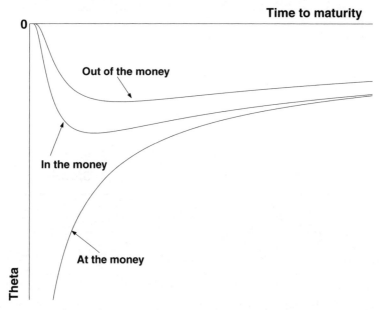

Figure 6.4 Variation of theta with time to maturity for a European call option.

money put option. This together with an interest rate advantage makes – as time passes – a far in-the-money European put option become more valuable. In Figure 6.5 the variation of theta with stock price is plotted for a European put option when the interest rate is strictly positive, and in Figure 6.6 when the interest rate is 0, which is the same as for the European call option.

Respectively, the next two formulae give the thetas of the European call and put option.

$$\theta_{\text{call,European}} = \frac{\partial c_t}{\partial t} = -\frac{S_t\, e^{-\frac{d_1^2}{2}}\sigma}{2\sqrt{2\pi}\sqrt{T-t}} - rK\, e^{-r(T-t)}N(d_2) \quad (6.4)$$

$$\theta_{\text{put,European}} = \frac{\partial p_t}{\partial t} = -\frac{S_t\, e^{-\frac{d_1^2}{2}}\sigma}{2\sqrt{2\pi}\sqrt{T-t}} + rK\, e^{-r(T-t)}N(-d_2) \quad (6.5)$$

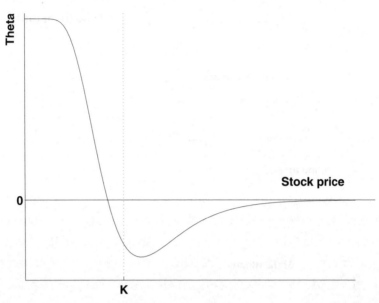

Figure 6.5 Variation of theta with stock price for a European put option, when the interest rate is strictly positive.

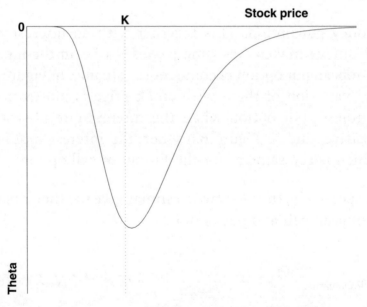

Figure 6.6 Variation of theta with stock price for a European call and put option, when the interest rate is zero.

Again, in these formulae it is really important that σ, r and $T - t$ are expressed in the same unit of time.

6.3 VEGA

Vega measures how sensitive the option price is to changes in volatility, while all other variables remain unchanged. So, it specifies how much the price of the option would change if there is a 1% change in volatility. In practice, vega is one of the most important measures of option risk, since option traders trade volatility. Option traders buy options at a certain implied volatility level in the expectation that this implied volatility will pick up, after which they can sell it at a higher implied volatility level. Or, if they think the implied volatility will decrease, they sell options at a certain implied volatility level hoping to buy it back at a lower implied volatility level. Note that – in interpreting vega – it is associated with implied volatility rather than a theoretical volatility, and this point will be elaborated on in Section 8.1. Also, for purposes of vega it does not matter whether the strategy involves call options or put options, because calls and puts have the same vega, see formulae (2.6) and (2.7) re-stated below:

$$\nu_{\text{call,European}} = \frac{\partial c_t}{\partial \sigma} = \frac{1}{\sqrt{2\pi}} e^{-\frac{d_1^2}{2}} S_t \sqrt{T - t} > 0 \quad (6.6)$$

$$\nu_{\text{put,European}} = \frac{\partial p_t}{\partial \sigma} = \frac{1}{\sqrt{2\pi}} e^{-\frac{d_1^2}{2}} S_t \sqrt{T - t} > 0 \quad (6.7)$$

The vega of any option will always be positive, which means that if (implied) volatility goes up every option

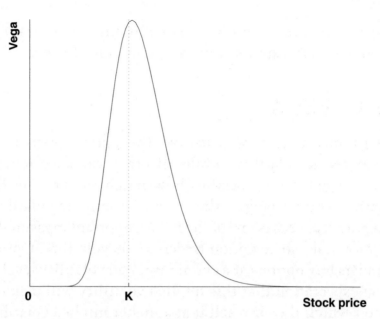

Figure 6.7   Variation of vega with stock price for a European call and put option.

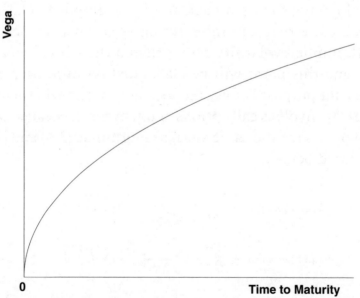

Figure 6.8   Variation of vega with time to maturity for a European call and put option.

will become more valuable. Respectively, Figures 6.7 and 6.8 give the variation of vega with respect to the stock price and the variation with respect to the time to maturity for a European option on a non-dividend paying stock. From these figures it is clear that vega is largest when the share is trading close to the strike price and the longer the term of the option the larger the vega. So, in comparing gamma and vega it is good to remember that both these variables are largest when the share is trading close to the strike price, but when considering the time to maturity, gamma is large when the term of the option is short, whereas vega is largest when the term of the option is long.

Chapter

7

....

THE PROFIT OF
OPTION TRADERS

As was shown in Section 5.1, an option can be hedged by selling δ[1] underlying stocks. That is, if an investor has a long position in an option, and during the term of this option he has a constant short position of δ underlying stocks, the return on this portfolio is the interest rate. Since δ changes as the price of the underlying stock changes and with the passage of time, an investor who wants to execute this strategy has to adjust the number of shorted stocks continuously. In practice, this is not possible. The number of shorted stocks can only be adjusted at discrete points in time. This is called 'dynamic hedging', and whenever the number of shorted stocks is adjusted according to the value of δ, the portfolio is made delta-neutral. In this chapter the implications of dynamic hedging will be discussed, and it will be shown that dynamic hedging is exactly the reason option traders make a profit.

Throughout this section there might be examples where a non-integer number of stocks is bought or sold. This is practically impossible and is just for the sake of argument.

7.1 DYNAMIC HEDGING OF A LONG CALL OPTION

Consider a stock which has a price of $10. The price of a call option on this stock with a strike price of $12 is $4.

---

[1] Since the δ of a put option is negative, this effectively means buying $|\delta|$ underlying stocks.

The delta of this particular call option is 0.40, the gamma is 0.02 and the theta is −0.01 per day. The following portfolio is put together:

- long 1 call option for $4;
- short 0.40 stocks for $10 each.

The aim of this section is to identify the profit of this portfolio for the following price trend of the underlying stock, when the portfolio is made delta-neutral every dollar and every 2 dollars, respectively:

- day 0 $10
- day 1 $9
- day 2 $8
- day 3 $9
- day 4 $10

7.1.1 Hedging dynamically every $1

- After 4 days the price of the stock is $10 again, which means that, apart from the effect of theta, the price of the call option is $4. But, because of theta, the call option depreciates 0.01 every day. So, after 4 days the call option is only worth $3.96.[2] Hence, the incurred loss on the call option is $0.04.
- Hedging dynamically every $1 gives the following cash flows. Because γ is 0.02, to make the position delta-neutral 0.02 stocks have to be bought if the stock price

---

[2] The fact that theta also changes with the passage of time is not taken into account here.

goes down by $1, and 0.02 stocks have to be sold if the stock price goes up by $1:[3]

- ○ 0.02 stocks bought for $9 on day 1;
- ○ 0.02 stocks bought for $8 on day 2;
- ○ 0.02 stocks sold for $9 on day 3;
- ○ 0.02 stocks sold for $10 on day 4.

Hence, the profit of dynamic hedging is $0.04.

For this particular hedging scheme and price trend of the stock, the total profit of this portfolio is $0.

7.1.2 Hedging dynamically every $2

- After 4 days the price of the stock is $10 again, which means that, apart from the effect of theta, the price of the call option is $4. But, because of theta, the call option depreciates 0.01 every day. So, after 4 days the call option is only worth $3.96. Hence, the incurred loss on the call option is $0.04.
- Because the portfolio is hedged dynamically every $2, the portfolio is made delta-neutral on day 2 and day 4. Remembering that a γ of 0.02 means that if the stock price goes down by $1 delta goes down by 0.02, it is clear that on day 2, $2 \times 0.02 = 0.04$ stocks have to be bought to make the portfolio delta-neutral. In the same way, on day 4 0.04 stocks have to be sold to make the portfolio delta-neutral. This leads to the following

---

[3] The fact that delta also changes with the passage of time is not taken into account here.

cash flows:

- ○ 0.04 stocks bought for $8 on day 2;
- ○ 0.04 stocks sold for $10 on day 2.

So, the profit of dynamic hedging is $0.08.

For this particular hedging scheme and price trend of the stock, the total profit of this portfolio is $0.04.

These two numerical examples show that, when hedging a long call option dynamically, it is more profitable to make the portfolio delta-neutral after big stock price changes than after small stock price changes. However, this strategy bears a bigger risk. For example, the next price trend of the stock still gives a profit on dynamic hedging when done every $1, but when done every $2 it does not give a profit at all:

- • day 0 $10
- • day 1 $9
- • day 2 $8.50
- • day 3 $9
- • day 4 $10

7.2   DYNAMIC HEDGING OF A SHORT CALL OPTION

Again, consider a stock which has a price of $10. The price of a call option on this stock with a strike price of $12 is $4. The delta of this particular call option is 0.40, the gamma is 0.02, and the theta is −0.01 per day. The following portfolio is put together:

- short 1 call option for $4;
- long 0.40 stocks for $10 each.

The aim of this section is to identify the profit of this portfolio for the following price trend of the underlying stock, when the portfolio is made delta-neutral every dollar and every 2 dollars, respectively:

- day 0 $10
- day 1 $9
- day 2 $8
- day 3 $9
- day 4 $10

7.2.1 Hedging dynamically every $1

- After 4 days the price of the stock is $10 again, which means that, apart from the loss in time value, the price of the call option is $4. But, because of theta, the call option depreciates 0.01 every day. So, after 4 days the call option is only worth $3.96.[4] Because the call option was shorted, the profit on the call option is $0.04.
- Hedging dynamically every $1 gives the following cash flows. Because γ is 0.02 and the call option is shorted, to make the position delta-neutral, 0.02 stocks have to be sold if the stock price goes down by $1, and 0.02

---

[4] The fact that theta also changes with the passage of time is not taken into account here.

stocks have to be bought if the stock price goes up by $1:[5]

○ 0.02 stocks sold for $9 on day 1;
○ 0.02 stocks sold for $8 on day 2;
○ 0.02 stocks bought for $9 on day 3;
○ 0.02 stocks bought for $10 on day 4.

The loss because of dynamic hedging is $0.04.

For this particular hedging scheme and price trend of the stock, the total profit of this portfolio is $0. Although this profit is equal to the profit of the long call option, now the profit was made on the option and a loss was incurred on dynamic hedging, whereas with the long call option it was the other way around. The next example will show that the profit on the short call is minus the profit of the long call option whenever the same hedging scheme is used.

7.2.2 Hedging dynamically every $2

• After 4 days the price of the stock is $10 again, which means that, apart from the loss in time value, the price of the call option is $4. But, because of theta, the call option depreciates 0.01 every day. So, after 4 days the call option is only worth $3.96. Because the call option was shorted, the profit on the call option is $0.04.
• Because the portfolio is hedged dynamically every $2, the portfolio is made delta-neutral on day 2 and day 4.

---

[5] The fact that delta also changes with the passage of time is not taken into account here.

Remembering that a γ of 0.02 means that if the stock price goes down by \$1 delta goes down by 0.02, it is clear that for the shorted call on day 2, $2 \times 0.02 = 0.04$ stocks have to be sold to make the portfolio delta-neutral. In the same way, on day 4 0.04 stocks have to be bought to make the portfolio delta-neutral. This leads to the following cash flows:

○ 0.04 stocks sold for \$8 on day 2;
○ 0.04 stocks bought for \$10 on day 2.

So, the loss of dynamic hedging is \$0.08.

For this particular hedging scheme and price trend of the stock, the total loss of this portfolio is \$0.04.

The foregoing examples show that whenever the same hedging scheme is used the profit of the short call is minus the profit of the long call. Moreover, for a long call option it is more profitable to make the portfolio delta-neutral after big stock price changes than after small stock price changes, whereas for a short call option it is more profitable to make the portfolio delta-neutral after small stock price changes.

7.3 PROFIT FORMULA FOR DYNAMIC HEDGING

In this section a formula is given that expresses the profit of dynamic hedging in terms of the change in stock price, after which the portfolio is made delta-neutral, and gamma. This formula will be derived for both the long call and the short call position in a situation of 0 interest rates. Derivation for the long put and short put is similar to the one given in this section.

Suppose the value of the underlying stock is S_t and the value of the call option is c_t. Suppose also that the delta of this call option is δ and the gamma of this call option is γ. Furthermore, assume the interest rate is equal to 0. The purpose of this section is to give a general formula of the profit on dynamic hedging, when this is done after a stock price movement of y dollars. It should be emphasized that such a formula only holds for really small stock price changes – that is, for really small y.

7.3.1   Long call option

- Upward stock movement:

  - Because of the long position in the call option a profit will be made on this option, since its price increases. Since the new delta after an upward stock movement of y is $\delta + \gamma y$, the average delta over the upward stock movement is:

  $$\frac{\delta + (\delta + \gamma y)}{2} \qquad (7.1)$$

    The increase in option price is equal to the average delta over the upward stock movement times the difference in stock price, which reads mathematically as:

  $$\frac{\delta + (\delta + \gamma y)}{2} \times y \qquad (7.2)$$

○ Because of the long position in the call option, there is a short position in δ underlying stocks (else the portfolio would not be delta-neutral). After the price of the stock has gone up by \$y, γy stocks have to be sold to make the portfolio delta-neutral again. So, a loss is incurred on the stocks, and it is equal to:

$$-\delta y \qquad (7.3)$$

The total profit of this dynamic hedge is

$$\frac{\gamma}{2} \times y^2 \qquad (7.4)$$

- Downward stock movement:
  ○ Because of the decrease in stock price, the value of the long call position decreases as well. The average delta over downward stock movement is:

$$\frac{\delta + (\delta - \gamma y)}{2} \qquad (7.5)$$

Because of the long position in the call option, the incurred loss on this option is:

$$\frac{\delta + (\delta - \gamma y)}{2} \times -y \qquad (7.6)$$

  ○ Because of the long position in the call option, there is a short position in δ underlying stocks (else the portfolio would not be delta-neutral). After the price of the stock has gone down by \$y, γy stocks have to be bought to make the portfolio delta-neutral again. So, a profit is made on the stocks, and it is equal to:

$$\delta y \tag{7.7}$$

Again, the total profit of the dynamic hedge is:

$$\frac{\gamma}{2} \times y^2 \tag{7.8}$$

In conclusion, whether the stock price goes up or down the profit from dynamic hedging a long call option after a small stock price change y is always equal to $\frac{\gamma}{2} \times y^2$.

7.3.2 Short call option

- Upward stock movement:

  o Because of the increase in stock price, the value of the short position in the call option decreases. The average delta over the upward stock movement is:

  $$\frac{\delta + (\delta + \gamma y)}{2} \tag{7.9}$$

  Because of the short position in the call option the incurred loss on this option is equal to:

  $$-\frac{\delta + (\delta + \gamma y)}{2} \times y \tag{7.10}$$

  o Because of the short position in the call option, there is a long position in δ underlying stocks (else the portfolio would not be delta-neutral). After the price of the stock has gone up by $\$y$, γy stocks have to be bought to make the portfolio delta-neutral again. So, a profit is made on the stocks, and it is equal to:

$$\delta y \qquad (7.11)$$

The total loss on this dynamic hedge is:

$$-\frac{\gamma}{2} \times y^2 \qquad (7.12)$$

- Downward stock movement:
  - ○ Because of the decrease in stock price, the value of the short position in the call option increases. The average delta over the downward stock movement is:

$$\frac{\delta + (\delta - \gamma y)}{2} \qquad (7.13)$$

Because of the short position in the call option the profit made on this call option is:

$$-\frac{\delta + (\delta - \gamma y)}{2} \times -y = \frac{\delta + (\delta - \gamma y)}{2} \times y \qquad (7.14)$$

  - ○ Because of the short position in the call option, there is a long position in δ underlying stocks (else the portfolio would not be delta-neutral). After the price of the stock has gone down by \$y, γy stocks have to be sold to make the portfolio delta-neutral again. So, a loss is made on the stocks, and it is equal to:

$$-\delta y \qquad (7.15)$$

Again, the total loss on the dynamic hedge is equal

to:
$$-\frac{\gamma}{2} \cdot y^2 \qquad (7.16)$$

In conclusion, whether the stock price goes up or down the profit from dynamic hedging a short call option after a small stock price change y is always equal to $-\frac{\gamma}{2} \times y^2$.

Similar to the derivations of the long call and the short call, the profit formulas of a dynamic hedge can be derived for the long put and short put. One will find that the profit formula for the long put is $\frac{\gamma}{2} y^2$ and for the short put $-\frac{\gamma}{2} y^2$. Again it should be emphasized that these formulae only hold for small values of y. It turns out that dynamic hedging of short call and put options leads to losses. This raises a logical question: Why would one want to hedge short positions in call and put options? The answer is easy for an American option. Because of dynamic hedging the position is made delta-neutral again, so should the option be exercised the loss will not be that big. For a European option it is also logical. It has been shown that, when holding a short position in either a call or a put, hedging dynamically after big stock price changes leads to bigger losses than if done after small stock price changes. So, to reduce the risk, the holder of a short position in a European option should hedge his position dynamically.

In conclusion, dynamic hedging of a long position in an option leads to a profit and compensates for the price paid for the option. An option trader who buys an option speculates on earning more by dynamic hedging than the price he has to pay for the option. Dynamic hedging of a short position in an option comes down to reducing the risk. An option trader who writes an option speculates on losing less on dynamic hedging than the price he gets for the option.

7.4 THE RELATIONSHIP BETWEEN DYNAMIC HEDGING AND θ

In the previous section it was derived that the profit from dynamic hedging of a long call option is $\frac{\gamma}{2} y^2$, provided the interest rate is 0. In this formula, y is the movement of the stock after which the portfolio is made delta-neutral. If σ is the volatility over a small time interval I, then the expected magnitude of movement of the stock in this time interval is equal to:

$$\sigma S_t \qquad (7.17)$$

So, when the portfolio is made delta-neutral after this time interval I, the expected movement of the stock will be σS_t. This means that, if the portfolio is made delta-neutral after a period of time equal to I, $y = \sigma S_t$ in the profit formula of dynamic hedging. Hence, the profit of dynamic hedging every time interval I is equal to:

$$\frac{\gamma \cdot \sigma^2 \cdot S_t^2}{2} \qquad (7.18)$$

Substituting the expression for γ – cf. equation (6.1) – into equation (7.18) gives the following expression for the profit of dynamic hedging every time interval I. Since σ is measured over a time interval I, the unit of $T - t$ should also be I:

$$\frac{e^{\frac{-d_1^2}{2}}\sigma S_t}{2\sqrt{2\pi}\sqrt{T-t}} \tag{7.19}$$

If the interest rate is 0, the expression for theta – cf. equation (6.4) – is equal to (the unit of time for σ and $T - t$ is I):

$$\theta_I = -\frac{e^{\frac{-d_1^2}{2}}\sigma S_t}{2\sqrt{2\pi}\sqrt{T-t}} \tag{7.20}$$

From equations (7.19) and (7.20) it can be concluded that, for a long call option, the profit of dynamic hedging every time interval I is expected to be as much as the incurred loss on the option per time period I.[6] It should be emphasized that this relation only holds if I is really small. The same derivation can be executed for a long put option.

------

[6] Although in this derivation it is not taken into account that δ also changes with the passage of time and θ changes with the stock price, this relation still holds. This is caused by the fact that these two effects are very small compared with the effect of γ and θ, respectively. After all, had this been taken into account, then the profit of the dynamic hedge would have been:

$$\left(\frac{\gamma}{2} \times y + \frac{\partial \delta}{\partial t}\right) \times y \overset{y=\sigma S_t}{=} \left(\frac{e^{\frac{-d_1^2}{2}}}{2\sqrt{2\pi}\sqrt{T-t}} + \frac{e^{\frac{-d_1^2}{2}}}{\sqrt{2\pi}}\left(\frac{\ln\left(\frac{S_t}{K}\right)}{2\sigma(T-t)\sqrt{T-t}} - \frac{\sigma}{4\sqrt{T-t}}\right)\right)\sigma S_t$$

Because σ is equal to some constant times $1/\sqrt{T-t}$, and $T - t$ is very big (the unit of time is I), the second term in brackets it negligibly small compared with the first term in brackets. This means the profit of a dynamic hedge of a long call option is $\dfrac{e^{\frac{-d_1^2}{2}}\sigma S_t}{2\sqrt{2\pi}\sqrt{T-t}}$. In the same way it can be argued that the loss in time value, after a time interval I, of a long call option is equal to $-\dfrac{e^{\frac{-d_1^2}{2}}\sigma S_t}{2\sqrt{2\pi}\sqrt{T-t}}$.

Of course, for a short position in either a call or a put option the reverse holds. That is, the profit comes from θ and the loss from dynamic hedging. So, from the above one sees that when the interest rate is 0, the following relationship holds between γ and θ:

$$\tfrac{1}{2}\sigma^2 S_t^2 \gamma + \theta = 0 \qquad (7.21)$$

This relationship only holds for an infinitesimally short period of time I and under the assumption that the actual volatility of the stock is equal to the implied volatility of the options. To see this last statement, remember that the option Greeks are all calculated with implied volatility as an input.

7.5   THE RELATIONSHIP BETWEEN DYNAMIC HEDGING AND θ WHEN THE INTEREST RATE IS STRICTLY POSITIVE

The aim of this section is to find a relationship between dynamic hedging and θ when the interest rate is strictly positive. In Section 7.4 it was shown that, when the interest rate is 0, the relation was that the expected profit or loss made on dynamic hedging was offset by the expected profit or loss made on the time value of the option, when the dynamic hedge was made after an infinitesimally small period of time I. In a way, this shows that the price of the option is fair. Mathematically, this can expressed by:

$$\tfrac{1}{2}\sigma^2 S_t^2 \gamma + \theta = 0 \qquad (7.22)$$

One would expect that, when the interest rate is strictly positive, the profit or loss made on dynamic hedging is still offset by the profit or loss of the time value of the option, provided the dynamic hedge is made after an infinitesimally small period of time I. This appears to be the case and can easily be shown from the derivations in Sections 7.3 and 7.4.

Consider an investor holding a long position in a call option. In Section 7.4 it was shown that the profit on a dynamic hedge after a small period of time I is:

$$\tfrac{1}{2}\sigma^2 S_t^2 \gamma = \frac{e^{-\frac{d_1^2}{2}}\sigma S_t}{2\sqrt{2\pi}\sqrt{T-t}}$$

When the interest rate is strictly positive, some additional terms need to be taken into account to get the total profit on the dynamic hedge. Because this investor holds a long position in the call option he not only loses money because of the theta but also because he could get interest on the value of the call option. This loss is equal to the interest rate over the time period I times the price of the option. Mathematically:[7]

$$-rc_t = -r\Big(S_t N(d_1) - K\, e^{-r(T-t)} N(d_2)\Big)$$

---

[7] In fact, this loss is actually equal to $-(e^r - 1)(S_t N(d_1) - K\, e^{-r(T-t)} N(d_2))$. But, when r is small (and this is the case since r is measured over the small period of time I), Taylor expansion gives that the loss is equal to $-r(S_t N(d_1) - K\, e^{-r(T-t)} N(d_2))$

where the unit of time of r is I, just like the unit of time of σ and $T - t$. Because this investor hedges his portfolio dynamically over the small period of time I, he has a short position in $\delta = N(d_1)$ underlying stocks. This means that he will receive interest on the value of the stock position, which is equal to:[8]

$$r\, \delta S_t = rN(d_1)S_t$$

So, when the interest rate is strictly positive, the total profit on the dynamic hedge after a small period of time I is equal to:

$$\frac{e^{\frac{-d_1^2}{2}}\sigma S_t}{2\sqrt{2\pi}\sqrt{T-t}} - r\left(S_t N(d_1) - K\,e^{-r(T-t)}N(d_2)\right) + rN(d_1)S_t$$

$$= \frac{e^{\frac{-d_1^2}{2}}\sigma S_t}{2\sqrt{2\pi}\sqrt{T-t}} + rK\,e^{-r(T-t)}N(d_2) \quad (7.23)$$

Because, when the interest rate is positive, the theta of a call option after a small period of time is equal to (the unit of time for σ, $T - t$ and r is I):

$$\theta_I = -\frac{e^{-d_1^2 2}\sigma S_t}{2\sqrt{2\pi}\sqrt{T-t}} - rK\,e^{-r(T-t)}N(d_2) \quad (7.24)$$

the profit on a dynamic hedge is again offset by the loss because of theta. Of course, the same derivation can be executed for the long put option. The derivation for the short call and short put option will give a reverse result. That is, the loss that is made on dynamic hedging after a

---

[8] Again, the actual profit is $(e^r - 1)N(d_1)S_t$, but by Taylor expansion it can be shown that this is equal to $rN(d_1)S_t$.

small period of time I is offset by the profit because of theta. Mathematically, the foregoing reads in terms of:

$$\frac{1}{2}\sigma^2 S_t^2 \gamma - rc_t + r\delta S_t + \theta = 0 \qquad (7.25)$$

$$\Updownarrow$$

$$\frac{1}{2}\sigma^2 S_t^2 \gamma + r\delta S_t + \theta = rc_t \qquad (7.26)$$

7.6 CONCLUSION

As shown in the previous sections, the expected profit or loss from dynamic hedging is negative the profit or loss because of theta, provided the option portfolio is hedged dynamically after an infinitesimally small period of time. Although this relation only holds for small periods of time, it is clear that, approximately, this will also hold for larger periods of time. It should be emphasized that this relation only holds if the stock appears to move according to implied volatility. And this is where the vision of an option trader comes in. If an option trader thinks implied volatility is too low, he should buy the option. If he is right he is *likely* to make a bigger profit from dynamic hedging (the profit formula for dynamic hedging of a long option increases in volatility) than the loss he incurs because of theta. If he thinks implied volatility is too high, he should write an option. If he is right his loss on dynamic hedging is *likely* to be less than the profit because of theta. It is important to bear in mind that being able to say whether implied volatility is too low or too high is no guarantee of making a profit. It really depends on after which move in the underlying the portfolio is made delta-neutral. This was shown in

Section 7.1. The magnitude of the profit also depends on at which point in time the stock realizes its biggest volatility and how close it is to 'at the money'. For example, consider a long position in an at-the-money call option expiring in 10 days' time. Since the gamma of an at-the-money call option increases as the option comes closer to maturity, it is easy to see from the profit formula of dynamic hedging – see equation (7.8) – that it is better to have a 10% move in the stock on the day before expiry than 10 days before expiry.

In conclusion, the profit of an option trader depends on two aspects. First of all, he has to judge whether implied volatility is too low or too high and, second, he has to make his portfolio delta-neutral after the right stock price movements and at the right points in time.

Chapter

8

OPTION GREEKS
IN PRACTICE

W hen trading options it is very important to understand the option Greeks, since this helps traders to understand the risk they are facing. Although the option Greeks primarily help traders to understand their risk, it also helps them to determine which strategies will benefit most from their view on a certain company or their view on the overall economy. The following sections will explain the option Greeks in more detail and will give a flavour for which strategies are most appropriate to benefit from certain company or economical events.

8.1   INTERACTION BETWEEN GAMMA AND VEGA

As mentioned in Section 6.3, gamma is large for options with a short time to maturity and vega is large for options with a long time to maturity. However, for both gamma and vega it is the case that they are largest for options close to 'at the money'. In summary, at-the-money options with a long time to maturity have large vegas and relatively small gammas, and at-the-money options with a short time to maturity have large gammas and relatively small vegas. So, when a trader wants to decide whether he should buy a long-dated or a short-dated option, he is basically deciding whether he wants to do a vega or a gamma trade.

In Chapter 7 it was shown that when buying an option the profit for the trader comes from movements in the underlying share, so that he is able to adjust his delta.

Every time the trader adjusts his delta, he is basically buying the underlying share at a low level and selling it at a high level. The reason that movements in the underlying share cause movements in delta is because of the gamma. So, if a trader thinks that a share will go through a volatile period in the next 3 months, after which the share will become less volatile, the best strategy is to buy a short-dated option. This will provide the trader with a large gamma, so that he will benefit most from the movements in the underlying share. This is a very popular strategy during the reporting season, since this is the time when companies give their results and outlook for the year, which can cause large movements in the underlying share.

Another strategy is to buy a long-dated option. As mentioned, a long-dated option has a small gamma and a large vega. So, in contrast to a short-dated option, when a trader buys a long-dated option he is not so much concerned with the realized volatility but more with the implied volatility. That is to say, when a trader buys a 3-year option he wants the 3-year implied volatility to pick up, after which he can sell the option at a better level. The reason that he is not concerned with the realized volatility in the near future is because a 3-year option has a tiny gamma, so he is not going to benefit much from adjusting the delta of this option. However, when the realized volatility picks up, the implied volatility of a 3-year option is likely to pick up as well, only not as much as the implied volatility of a 3-month option. This illustrates once more that, when a trader expects volatility to pick up in the near future, he is better off buying a short-dated option than a long-dated. From this it is clear that the only justification for buying a long-dated option is that the trader expects a big event in the medium to longer term. This event can be a war, an election, the oil price, a merger or virtually anything that is likely to move the share price.

The above makes it clear that understanding the option Greeks not only enables traders to manage their risk, but it also enables them to understand what strategy best suits their view on the economy. However, the above discusses two very simple strategies for two different economical events. In reality, traders will try to do spreads to give their view on the economy some gearing. For example, just before a reporting season one spread could be to buy a 1-month option and sell a 3-month option. This strategy will give some gearing to the view that the annual report will cause the share price to have a big one-off move, after which the share price will settle down and hardly move at all. Equally, to give gearing to the view that the share price will hardly move for the coming year after which a rise in oil prices will cause the share to go through a volatile year, the best strategy is to buy a 2-year option and sell a 1-year option.

This section only discussed the aspects of gamma and vega strategies under the assumption that the underlying share price will be close to the chosen strikes of the options throughout the whole term of the options. This is because, if the share price moves too far away from the strike price of an option, the option will have neither gamma nor vega. This issue will be addressed in Section 8.2

8.2 THE IMPORTANCE OF THE DIRECTION OF THE UNDERLYING SHARE TO THE OPTION GREEKS

The problem traders face when buying a long-dated option is that they do not know where the underlying share will be trading in, say, 2 years' time. This section will show why it is so important that a trader also needs to have a view on the direction of the stock when trading long-dated options rather than just having a view on the volatility of this stock.

Suppose an option trader buys an at-the-money option with an implied volatility of 25 expiring in 2 years' time. As shown in the previous section, this is a typical vega trade, meaning that the trader expects a pickup in implied volatility in the near future after which he can sell the option at a higher implied volatility level. Since the trader will have hedged his exposure to the underlying stock this strategy will make him a profit provided he is right about the pickup in implied volatility. However, let's suppose that this particular option is very illiquid, so it is highly unlikely that the trader will be able to sell the option on in the market. This means that the trader will be stuck with this particular option position for the life of the option. One would expect that, if the underlying share realizes a volatility of 25 over the life of the option, the trader will neither make nor lose money. Unfortunately, it is not as simple as that. Consider a scenario where the share price drifts away from the strike within 2 years in a low-volatile manner, after which it becomes very volatile causing the volatility over the life of the option to be exactly 25. In this scenario the trader will most definitely lose money. This is because when the share moves away from the strike the option will have little gamma left. As was shown in Chapter 7, a small gamma will cause the trader to adjust his delta relatively infrequently, in which case he will not make enough money from delta-hedging to earn back the premium paid for the option.

8.3   PIN RISK FOR SHORT-DATED OPTIONS

It might seem counterintuitive that one of the most risky options appears to be very short-dated at-the-money options. The problem with, say, a 1-day at-the-money option is that it will be hard to assess whether this option will expire in or out of the money. The direct result is that when an option trader decides to sell such a 1-day at-the-money call option he does not know what hedge to put against this option. Of course, the trader could look at the delta of this option and hedge accordingly, but because the option has such a large gamma the delta almost becomes meaningless. Inevitably, the trader will have to take a view on the underlying share price at expiration. In the case of an at-the-money call option the trader would have to assess whether the underlying share price will be higher than the strike at expiration, in which case he will hedge the call option with a one delta (buy the same number of shares as options), or lower than the strike, in which case he should hedge with a zero delta (do not buy any shares). Obviously, this strategy can be very costly if the trader is proved to be wrong. Even if the trader puts the trade on with a 50% delta (buy half the number of shares as options) it could still be a very costly strategy because of the large gamma. The reason the gamma is so large is because the delta will change from 0 to 1 or *vice versa* every time the underlying share price goes through the strike. This is what traders call 'pin risk', the underlying share price being exactly at the strike when the option almost expires.

8.4   THE RISKIEST OPTIONS TO GO SHORT

In a low-volatility environment implied volatilities usually trade at a premium to realized volatility. The result is that it looks attractive to go short options. However, there is quite a good reason for it to look so attractive. The premium one receives for shorting an option is to cover the event risk. To make this more clear, consider the following example. An option trader is considering to short an at-the-money 6-month option on Ahold. Ahold is the Dutch retailer that came into trouble after accounting scandals at some of its subsidiaries. After a large drop in the share price, causing the volatility of the stock to be extremely high, the volatility settled down. Suppose the 6-month historical volatility is currently 32% annualized (approximately 2% a day).

Although the 6-month historic volatility is 32% it is highly unlikely that anybody would want to short a 6-month option on Ahold for an implied volatility of 32%. The reason is that the chance of other irregularities at Ahold is just too high, which makes the chance of another big move in the near future quite considerable. Because of this high event risk the probability of the stock realizing more than 32% is just too high. Even if the stock were to realize less than 32% for most of the coming 6 months, and after one announcement of more irregularities it moves 10% taking the volatility over 6 months exactly to 32% annualized, the option trader would still lose money. The reason for this is that the losses on gamma-hedging are squarely related to the move in the underlying share – see formula (7.16). This means that twice as big a move results in four times as big a loss. In the case of Ahold moving 10% on 1 day, this would result in 25 times as big a loss because the average move is 2% a day.

However, if a trader has good fundamental reasons to believe that there will be no further irregularities at Ahold, the above phenomenon can also give him a good opportunity to make money. If he shorts the option and there are no further scandals he will have been paid a premium in terms of volatility that will not be realized.

Chapter

9

....

SKEW

W hen trading options one needs to be familiar with the phenomenon of 'skew'. At first, skew is something that is difficult to grasp, but it is perfectly explicable. This chapter gives the definition of skew and gives the reasons for it.

9.1   WHAT IS SKEW?

Skew is very much related to implied volatility, which is explained in Chapter 4. Chapter 4 explained that, given the price of a specific option in the options market, one can calculate the implied volatility of this option. It appears to be the case that options with lower strike prices have higher implied volatilities. That is to say, that the 'market' prices options with lower strike prices relatively more expensive than options with higher strike prices. The phenomenon where options with lower strike prices have higher implied volatilities is called 'skew'. So, when two 3-month options on Royal Dutch/Shell are compared, one with a strike price of $40 and one with a strike price of $32, the one with the strike price of $32 will most definitely have a higher implied volatility. This sounds odd considering that both options are expiring in 3 months' time and, as mentioned in Chapter 4, the implied volatility is the market's expectation of the realized volatility of Royal Dutch/Shell in the 3 months ahead on which the strike price has no influence. The reasons for skew will be explained in Section 9.2.

9.2   REASONS FOR SKEW

There are two main reasons for skew which have to be named together, because one or the other still does not explain skew. First of all, as long as stock markets exist the experience is that when stock markets are going down they are more volatile than when stock markets go up. This still does not explain why an option with a lower strike price should have a higher implied volatility than an option with a higher strike price, since for both options the realized volatility goes up by the same amount. Apparently, this downward movement followed by a pickup in volatility has a bigger impact on the option with the lower strike price than on the one with the higher strike price. The reason for this is that when the stock is going down it moves away from the higher strike price and closer to the lower strike price which, as was shown in Section 6.1, causes the option with the lower strike price to get a larger gamma. According to Chapter 7 this, in turn, means that the (low-strike) option delta has to be re-hedged more frequently resulting in a larger loss for the investor who sold the low-strike option. Naturally, the seller of a low-strike option wants to get compensated for this phenomenon, which will cause the investor to 'charge' a higher implied volatility for the lower strike option such that he gets a relatively higher premium for a lower strike option than for a higher strike option.

9.3 REASONS FOR HIGHER VOLATILITIES IN FALLING MARKETS

As stated in Section 9.2, it is the case that when share prices are going down they become more volatile, which ultimately causes skew. The reason for this is that when share prices are going down investors are getting more uncertain about the future and tend to panic. In this perspective it is good to compare volatility with uncertainty; when there is a lot of uncertainty share prices tend to be more volatile, whereas when there is a lot of certainty share prices move in a very unvolatile manner. Another less scientific and distinct reason, which plays possibly a less significant role, is that although a share price is going down investors still think in absolute movements, which, of course, causes higher volatility as this is measured in percentages.

Chapter

10

....

SEVERAL OPTION STRATEGIES

The most popular option strategies amongst investors usually involve more than just buying or selling an option outright. In this chapter several different option strategies will be explained. Why investors would execute these option strategies is discussed from a break-even point of view.

10.1 CALL SPREAD

One of the most popular strategies is the call spread. A call spread involves nothing more than two calls, one with a low strike and another with a higher strike. An investor is said to be 'buying the call spread' if he buys the lower strike and sells the higher strike. 'Selling the call spread' means selling the lower strike and buying the higher one. Buying the call spread is called a 'bullish strategy' because the investor benefits if the underlying increases in value. However, the investor's profits are capped because he has sold another call with a higher strike to fund his bullish view on the stock. As an example, consider an investor who buys an at-the-money call on BMW and partially funds this by selling a 120% call on BMW. In this case the investor will profit from an increase in BMW's share price up to the point where the share price has reached 120% of its initial value. Every percentage gain over 20% will not make the investor any money, hence his profits are capped. When the two payoff profiles of a long at-the-money call option and a short 120% call option are combined, one gets the payoff graph in Figure 10.1.

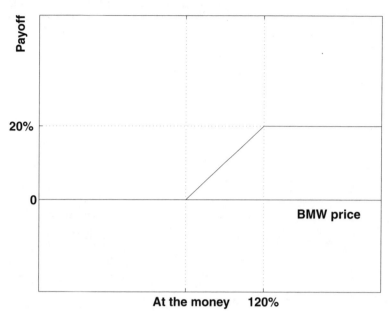

Figure 10.1 Payoff profile at maturity for an at-the-money/120% call spread on BMW.

10.2 PUT SPREAD

A put spread is the opposite of a call spread in that when an investor buys a put spread he is executing a 'bearish strategy', whereas buying a call spread is a bullish strategy. Buying a put spread means buying a higher strike put and selling a lower strike put. Since a put with a higher strike is always more expensive than a put with a lower strike and the same maturity, the investor will have to pay a premium to put this strategy on. When an investor buys a put spread he partially funds his bearish view on the underlying stock by selling a lower strike put. However, by partially funding his bearish view he is also limiting the profits of his strategy, because the investor only benefits from the stock going down, up to the strike

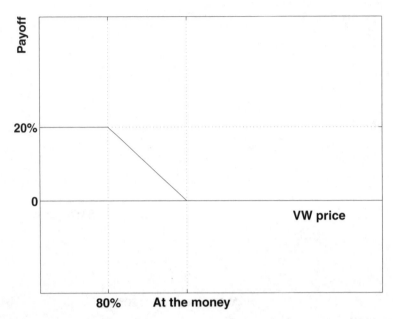

Figure 10.2   Payoff profile at maturity for an at-the-money/80% put spread on Volkswagen.

of the downside put. As an example, consider an investor who buys an at-the-money put on Volkswagen (VW) and partially funds this by selling an 80% put on VW. In this case the investor will profit from a decline in VW's share price up to the point where it has reached 80% of its initial value. If the share price drops below 80% of its initial value the investor will not benefit any longer. Again, when the two payoff profiles of a long at-the-money put and a short 80% put are combined, one gets the payoff graph in Figure 10.2. It is important to understand that the payoff in Figure 10.2 is not the investor's profit because he would have paid an initial premium to put this strategy on. So, if this strategy cost him 2% of the initial share price the investor will only start making money if the share price drops below 98% of the initial share price. However, had he just bought an at-the-money put it would have cost him considerably more – for example, 5% – and, therefore, the share price would have to drop below 95% of the initial share price before the investor would start making money. Obviously, the put outright would not limit his upside potential to 18% but in theory to 95% if the share price goes to 0.

10.3   COLLAR

The collar or 'risk reversal' is used to give gearing to a certain view on the underlying rather than limiting the upside potential of that strategy, as for the call or put spread. A collar consists of a call with a higher strike and a put with a lower strike. If an investor is very bullish on a stock and he thinks the downside for the stock is very limited he could buy an upside call and sell a downside put to partially fund this strategy. However, the investor might not be limiting his upside potential when the stock goes up, but by selling the put he does expose himself to the stock going down. So, the investor is said to be 'gearing' his view because he can actually lose more than his investment when the stock ends up lower than the strike of the put. If an investor is bearish on a stock he could buy a downside put and sell an upside call to fund his view partially or in full, but therefore exposes himself to the stock price going up. Whether an investor is paying or receiving money to put on a risk reversal strategy depends on the forward and the skew. It is therefore ambiguous to talk about buying or selling a risk reversal.

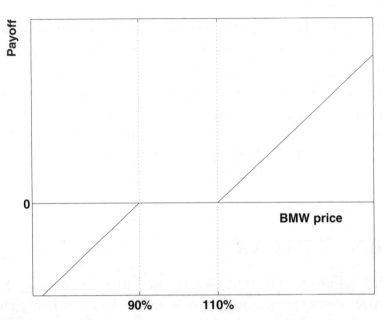

Figure 10.3 Payoff profile at maturity for a 90%/110% collar on BMW.

Consider an investor who is very bullish on BMW's share price and, therefore, wants to buy a 1-year 110% call. He also thinks that if the share price goes down it will not go down more than 10% in the coming year. Therefore, he wants to fund his 110% call by selling a 90% put with the same maturity. By combining the payoff profile of a long 110% call with a short 90% put, one would get the graph in Figure 10.3. Again, it is important to remember that Figure 10.3 does not show the profit profile of the investor. The profit depends on how much the investor received or paid for putting this 90%/110% collar on in the first place. If BMW's dividend yield is higher than the risk-free interest rate, the investor will most definitely have received money for this strategy. This is because, if the dividend yield is higher than the risk-free interest rate, the 1-year forward is less than 100% of the initial share price which will make the 1-year 90% put more valuable than the 1-year 110% call. On top of that, the skew will make the 90% put even more valuable and the 110% call less valuable.

Another feature of the collar is that it has a relatively high delta, because if a trader buys a put he needs to buy shares to hedge himself and if the trader also sells a call he needs to buy even more shares in order to be delta-hedged. Because of this high delta the collar can also be used to express a dividend view. If a trader thinks BMW is likely to increase its dividends, he will quite happily take the other side of the investor's strategy to buy the put and sell the call. Because, if BMW does increase its dividends, the forward should have been lower than the forward with the current dividends and the put will therefore increase in value and the call decrease in value.

10.4   STRADDLE

The straddle is a very popular strategy for investors who think the underlying stock will move away from its current level but do not know whether it will be up or down. A straddle consists of a call option and a put option with the same strike and same maturity. Since buying a straddle means buying both a call and a put option, the underlying needs to move away from the strike price considerably for the strategy to make money. For that very same reason, selling a 1-year at-the-money straddle is a very attractive strategy for investors who think the underlying will move sideways for the coming year. Since the investor will take in the premium of the straddle, he will most likely have to pay very little at maturity because the stock will not have moved away much from current levels. So, on either the put or the call the payout will be nothing and on the other one it will be very little.

As an example, consider an investor who knows that TomTom, the maker of car navigation systems, is due to come out with a statement which will be a real share mover. However, the investor does not know whether it will affect the share price positively or negatively. For that reason he decides to buy a 6-month at-the-money straddle on TomTom. Combining the two payoff profiles of a long at-the-money call and a long at-the-money put one will get Figure 10.4. To show the difference between the payoff of buying an at-the-money straddle on Tom-Tom and the profit of buying this straddle, suppose the investor paid $3 for the at-the-money straddle on Tom-Tom and the share price is currently trading at $20. The profit profile at maturity of buying an at-the-money straddle on TomTom would look like Figure 10.5.

10.5   STRANGLE

The strangle is very similar to the straddle with the difference that the call and the put do not have the same strike. So, a strangle consists of a call with a higher strike and a put with a lower strike. Therefore, like the straddle, the strangle is also of use to investors who think that the underlying share will move away from current levels. However, an investor might prefer a 90%/110% strangle

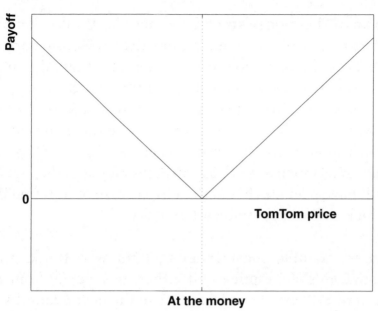

Figure 10.4   Payoff profile at maturity for a long at-the-money straddle on TomTom.

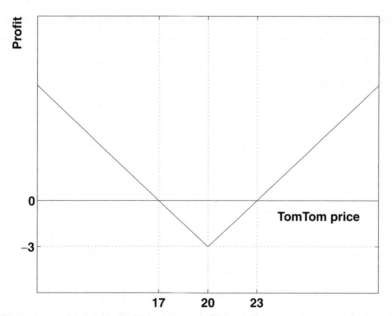

Figure 10.5   Payoff profile at maturity for a long at-the-money straddle on TomTom.

to an at-the-money straddle because he thinks that the share price will move much more than 10% from current levels but he wants to minimize his loss in case the share price does not move at all. By using the strangle to support his view his initial investment is much less than when buying an at-the-money straddle. If the share does move much more than 10% from current levels he will profit almost as much as with an at-the-money straddle, but he will have paid much less than in the case of the straddle, which makes his strategy less risky.

As an example consider an investor who thinks that TomTom's share price will either move away from its current $20 level by at least 20% in the next 6 months or not do anything at all. Instead of buying an at-the-money straddle where the initial investment is large and – in the case of a big move – the profit at maturity is large as well, the investor decides to buy a 6-months 90%/110% strangle where the initial investment is small and – in the case of a big move – the profit is almost as big as for the straddle. The payoff profile at maturity for this strategy is shown in Figure 10.6. To see that this strategy is less risky than buying a 6-month at-the-money straddle, suppose the investor paid $1.50 for the strangle and, as per the example in Section 10.4, he would have to pay $3 for the at-the-money straddle. If the share price were to move down by 20% TomTom's share price will be $16. The strangle would therefore make a profit of $0.50 (the strike of the 90% put is $18 and therefore makes $2 on this put) and the straddle would make a profit of $1. The two different profit profiles of the straddle and strangle are shown in Figure 10.7. Figure 10.7 clearly shows that the

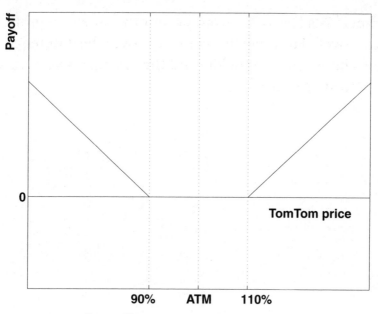

Figure 10.6   Profit profile at maturity for a long 90%/110% strangle on TomTom.

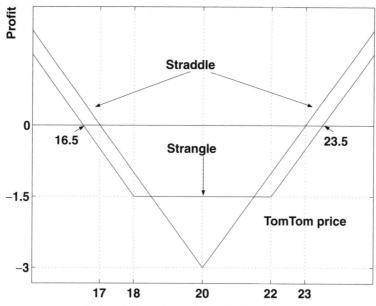

Figure 10.7   Profit profiles at maturity for a long 90%/110% strangle and an at-the-money straddle on TomTom.

strangle is a less risky strategy, but the potential profit is less as well. However, for very big moves the difference in profit between the straddle and the strangle is very small in percentage terms.

Chapter

11

DIFFERENT OPTION
STRATEGIES AND
WHY INVESTORS
EXECUTE THEM

Other than traders who trade options proprietary, there are basically two types of option investors, portfolio managers and corporates. In general, portfolio managers execute strategies to get a good return on their investments whereas corporates tend to invest in options to hedge a certain exposure. This chapter discusses which strategies are typical for the aforementioned investors and what they are looking to achieve.

11.1 THE PORTFOLIO MANAGER'S APPROACH TO OPTIONS

The difference between a portfolio manager and an option trader is that a portfolio manager usually has a view on the underlying share and buys or sells options to give this view some gearing whereas an option trader usually only has a view on the volatility of the underlying share. However, as shown in Section 8.2 it is important that the trader has a view on the direction of the stock when trading long-dated options.

Consider the situation when a pension fund sees a lot of upside potential for the stock Daimler Chrysler (DCX) in the next 2 years, and suppose DCX is currently trading at $40. Suppose that the pension fund thinks that DCX will be trading at $50 in 2 years' time. Rather than just buying the share DCX, the pension fund could buy a call option on DCX with a strike price of $40 for a price of $5 to improve the return-on-investment ratio. The reasoning being that if the pension fund buys 1,000 shares today it will cost the pension fund $40,000 to give an expected payoff of $50,000, whereas buying 5,000 options DCX with a strike price of $40 for $5 each will give the same expected payoff of $50,000 having only cost $25,000. In the first case the return on the investment is 25% over 2 years; in the second one it is 100% over 2 years.

11.2 OPTIONS AND CORPORATES WITH CROSS-HOLDINGS

The majority of large companies have cross-holdings – that is to say, they own shares in other companies. The reason for this is that companies want to diversify their risk and at the same time they are looking for a good return on this investment. What usually happens is that a large company buys a certain number of shares in another company already knowing at what level it wants to dispose its stake in that company. As a real life example, Daimler Chrysler (DCX) thinks that Asia will be the biggest growth area for the car industry in the next 5 years. Since DCX sells cars to customers at the top end of the range and the average income per person in Asia is still far below that in the U.S. and Europe, it is unlikely that DCX will benefit much from the potential growth in Asia. However, other car manufacturers are likely to see big growth in Asia which could dampen DCX's overall market share in the world's car industry. This could even jeopardize DCX's market share in the luxury car industry since other car manufacturers will get a stronger balance sheet than DCX's. This means it is of crucial importance that DCX breaks into Asia. Since

DCX's cars are too expensive for the average Asian, they need to buy a stake in another car manufacturer. So, as DCX actually did, it bought a stake in Mitsubishi Motors. Suppose DCX is looking to get a 50% return on this investment over the next 5 years. One strategy it could have executed is to sell 150% strike calls expiring in 5 years on these Mitsubishi shares.[1] This is a very attractive strategy to DCX since, if Mitsubishi shares do not go up by 50%, DCX will still have received the premium of the call options. However, if the Mitsubishi shares go up more than 50%, DCX will only receive 50% since the call options will get exercised against DCX; however, this is still no problem to DCX because it was only looking to make a return of 50%. So, this strategy ensures that DCX will still get some money even if the Mitsubishi shares do not go up by the desired 50%.

11.3   OPTIONS IN THE EVENT OF A TAKEOVER

Options can be very useful in a takeover situation, since the shareholders of the company being acquired are usually at least partially paid in shares of the acquiring company. Especially when a shareholder of the company being acquired is rather large, there is usually a period where this shareholder is not allowed to dispose of the received shares of the acquiring company. This means

---

[1] In practice, this strategy could only have been executed on a small part of DCX's stake in Mitsubishi since the equity derivatives markets are too small to cope with such a big stake.

that, even if this shareholder just wants to convert the shares of the acquiring company into cash, he cannot do so for a certain period. So, this shareholder finds himself in a situation where he owns shares in a company he cannot materialize for a certain period and, therefore, is fully exposed to the share price of this acquiring company over the specified period. Since this shareholder is only interested in receiving the cash for his holding in the acquiring company, he could hedge his exposure by buying downside put options on his shareholdings while funding this by selling upside call options in this company and, therefore, giving up some of the upside of his shareholdings, which he was not interested in, anyway. This strategy, where the investor buys downside puts and sells upside calls to fund it for no initial premium, is called a 'zero cost collar'. This is clearly a very attractive strategy to the investor. As an example, suppose BP takes over a Russian oil company with one big shareholder. The agreed takeover price is £250 million to be paid out in BP shares. Since it would disrupt BP's share price too much if the shares were to be sold in the market straight away, the investor can only start selling the BP shares after 6 months' time. To protect his BP holding, the Russian shareholder decides to enter into a zero cost collar with an investment bank for 50 million underlying shares (the price of one BP share is £5) with a maturity of 6 months. For this collar to be worth 0, the strikes need to be 90% for the put and 107% for the call. In this case the Russian shareholder has protected himself against a drop in BP's share price of more than 10% by giving up everything over 7% of the upside in BP's share price.

Just like the above example, the break-evens of the zero cost collar never look particularly attractive due to the effect of skew, which causes an investor to pay relatively more for a downside put than an upside call. However, zero cost collars on companies with low dividend yields can look attractive since the forwards on such companies are relatively high, making the puts less expensive and the calls more expensive.

11.4   RISK REVERSALS FOR INSURANCE COMPANIES

Insurance companies tend to execute the same strategy as described in Section 11.3, buying downside puts and selling upside calls, the so-called 'collar' or 'risk reversal'. The reason is that insurance companies have large exposures to stock markets, while at the same time having risk limits as to how much they can lose, were a stock market to go down by more than 10%. Whenever an insurance company gets close to these limits it tends to buy downside puts on an index and funds this partially or in full by selling upside calls on this same index. This strategy is called a 'risk reversal' or a 'collar'. For example, if the French insurance company AXA gets close to exceeding its exposure to the UK stock market, the obvious strategy is to buy a 90% put on the FTSE[2] index while selling a 107% call on the FTSE index for zero cost.

---

[2] The FTSE index is a weighted index of the largest UK stocks.

11.5 PRE-PAID FORWARDS

A strategy that is particularly popular in the United States among high net worth individuals and small to midcap companies that own stakes in other companies is the pre-paid forward. The principle is fairly straightforward and involves nothing more than a loan, a put option and a call option. Again, the easiest way to explain a pre-paid forward is by means of an example.

Consider an entrepreneurial farmer who has set up his own fizzy drink brand and is starting to market it throughout the United States. Because this fizzy drink is starting to get really popular in the United States, Coca-Cola feels threatened by this success and decides to offer the entrepreneurial farmer $100 million. However, the farmer will get paid in Coca-Cola shares and is not allowed to sell these shares for the coming year, because Coca-Cola wants to make sure that he will still be involved in the management and marketing of his fizzy drink for this 1-year period. Since the farmer is very entrepreneurial he already has a new idea of setting up his own dairy company. However, in order to do this he estimates that he needs $85 million as an investment. Since he is not allowed to sell his $100 million worth of Coca-Cola shares he basically wants to protect the value of his Coca-Cola shareholdings and he wants to get $85 million up front. To protect his Coca-Cola holdings he can buy a put and sell a call, either with the same strike price (e.g., at the money) or he could buy a lower strike put and a higher strike call in which case it is nothing more than a collar. Because he owns the shares he can get a cheap loan if he gives the underlying shares as collateral. A cheap loan means that the investor can borrow at, say, Libor[3] + 15 basis points[4] rather than Libor + 2%. If the investor puts the call, the put and the loan together as a package, it is called a 'pre-paid forward'. The question now becomes: How much is an investment bank prepared to give as a cheap loan? The answer lies in how the shares change hands at maturity and if the investment bank is still able to get repaid on the loan were the investor to default on it. Suppose the investor buys a 90% put and sells a 112% call on Coca-Cola for zero cost. Rather than giving the investor $85 million and charging the investor an interest rate of Libor + 15 bps a year, the investment bank will give the present value of $90 million where the discount factor is $\frac{1}{\text{Libor} + 15\text{bps}}$ and will get back $90 million at the end. Economically, this is exactly the same. But, more importantly, the reason that the investment bank is only comfortable with lending the discounted value of $90 million is to protect itself against a possible default of the loan. To see this, consider the situation where after 1 year the farmer defaults on the $90 million loan and Coca-Cola's share price has decreased by 20% to 80% of the current share price. At first sight, this seems really bad for the investment bank since it holds the shares as collateral, the value of which has decreased to $80 million and for that reason the bank will lose $10 million. How-

---

[3] Libor stands for 'London interbank offered rate' and is established every day by a group of banks and gives the rate at which banks are prepared to lend each other money overnight.
[4] 1 basis point is $\frac{1}{100}$ of 1%.

ever, under the agreement of the 90% put, the investment bank owes the farmer $10 million on which the investment bank will obviously default, making up for its $10 million loss. So, even if the farmer defaults on the loan the investment bank will still be able to collect the money for the loan if the share price drops below the strike of the put. If the share price does not drop below the strike of the put the collateral will be enough to cover for the money of the loan in case of default by the farmer. For this reason the investment bank can never be owed more at maturity than that percentage of collateral which is equal to the percentage strike of the put. This means that the investment bank is comfortable with giving an up-front amount of money that is equal to the present value of the percentage strike of the put times the value of the shares held as collateral. Assuming that USD Libor is equal to 2.5% the farmer will get an amount equal to $\frac{90}{1.0265} \times 90 = \$87.677$ million up front.

For the pre-paid forward type of structures, banks with a high credit rating have a significant advantage over banks with a lower rating. This is because banks with a higher rating can borrow at Libor flat whereas banks with a lower rating can only borrow at, say, Libor + 15 bps. Especially for longer dated structures, higher rated banks will be able to offer a much more attractive up-front payment. Typically, investment banks have lower ratings than retail banks. So, in this area retail banks have a significant advantage over investment banks, although investment banks are typically more aggressive in option structures.

11.6 EMPLOYEE INCENTIVE SCHEMES

Employee incentive schemes are getting more and more common nowadays. The idea behind these schemes is to stimulate employees by letting them benefit from the upside of the share price. This can be achieved by paying out a part of the employee's salary or bonus in call options on the share price of the company. This way of stimulating employees is particularly common for senior management.

11.7 SHARE BUY-BACKS

Large companies usually own their own stock, which is being held on their balance sheets as treasury stock. Within a certain range they will also have a mandate to buy their own stock. When a company has a share buy-back programme in place it will typically sell puts on its own stock with a strike at which it is comfortable buying. This means that the company receives an initial premium for the put. At maturity the company will either have to buy its own shares at the put option's strike price if the share price has dropped below the strike or the company gets to keep the put premium if the share price is above the strike. Obviously, this is a very attractive strategy to the company. Rather than just buying the shares in the market outright, it exploits the fact that option traders look at options in terms of volatility instead of break-evens and are therefore willing to pay a premium for this strategy. Typically, this has a dampening effect on the implied volatility of this specific stock since investment banks will get long put options on this stock and will try to sell it out in the market place.

Chapter
12

....

TWO EXOTIC
OPTIONS

Another class of options that is becoming increasingly important in the investment banking industry is the so-called 'exotic option'. The reason that this type of option is called an 'exotic option' is because the variables that determine the price of this option are not only the usual variables like stock price, strike price, interest rate, dividend and stock volatility but also variables like foreign exchange (FX) volatility or correlation between the stock price and a specific foreign exchange rate. In other words, when an investment bank executes a deal that involves an exotic option both the client as well as the investment bank expose themselves to more variables than when executing a deal involving only a plain vanilla option.

This chapter will only discuss two types of exotic options: the quanto option and the composite option.

12.1   THE QUANTO OPTION

The quanto option is designed for investors who want to execute an option strategy on a foreign stock but are only interested in the percentage return of that strategy and want to get paid this return in their own currency. The basic principle of a quanto option is that the exchange rate will be fixed to the prevailing exchange rate at inception of the option transaction and the payout of the quanto option will be this exchange rate times the payout of the regular option.

Consider a U.S. investor who is very bullish on the share price of BP (British Petroleum). For that reason this U.S.

investor wants to buy an at-the-money call option on BP expiring in 1 year. However, he does not want to get his return in British pounds but in US dollars. Assume that BP's share price is £5, the exchange rate is currently $2 per pound and in 1 year's time the share price is worth £5.50. The quanto at-the-money call option will give the U.S. investor a payout at maturity of $1 regardless of the change in exchange rate. In other words, the investor would expect a 10% return in U.S. dollars on the USD notional[1] amount he bought calls on, since BP's share price has increased by 10%.

From the above example it is clear that it is relatively easy to structure a quanto option; however, it is much harder to see what effect it has on how this option should be priced and what variables it depends on.

To see how this option should be priced, two new variables have to be introduced. The first variable is the correlation between BP's stock price and the foreign exchange, FX, rate. To get a better understanding of how this correlation affects the price of a quanto call option, an interesting question is whether the US investor who is buying an ATM USD quanto call is short or long correlation. Here, 'short correlation' means that the investor will benefit (quanto option will increase in value) if the correlation goes down and will lose in case the correlation goes up. The reverse holds for being long correlation. To answer this question, assume the correlation is positive, which means that if the British pound becomes

---

[1] 'Notional' is defined as the number of options times the current share price.

more valuable against the U.S. dollar, BP's share will go up. Now, one can easily see that the investor is short correlation (selling correlation), because if the British pound goes up the correlation aspect will cause the share price to go up and, therefore, the dollar increase of a plain vanilla call option is more than the dollar increase of a USD quanto call option, which has a fixed exchange rate. Similar analysis shows that if the British pound goes down, the correlation aspect will cause the share price to go down and the combination of a lower share price and a less valuable pound causes the dollar loss of a plain vanilla at-the-money call option to be less than the dollar loss of an at-the-money USD quanto call option. To put it differently, if the correlation goes down from, say, 1 to −1 the holder of a USD quanto call option will benefit, since he is better off holding a plain vanilla call option if the correlation is 1 whereas if the correlation is −1 he is better off holding a USD quanto call option. The above example shows that the holder of a USD quanto call is short correlation; however, when extending this analysis to a USD quanto put one will find that the holder of such an option is long correlation.

The second variable is FX volatility. For this variable it is less obvious whether the US investor is long or short this FX volatility. At this point it is good to introduce a model that describes the stock price difference in U.S. dollars for a small time interval. This model shows under which circumstances a quanto option is long or short FX volatility and further shows once more why the holder of a quanto call is short correlation and the holder of a quanto put is long correlation.

The model most commonly used for modelling a share price on a non-dividend paying stock is the Black–Scholes model which describes the difference in stock price for a small time interval. The formula is as follows[2]:

$$\frac{dS_t}{S_t} = r \, dt + \sigma_S \, dW_t \qquad (12.1)$$

where S_t = Stock price at time t;
   r = Risk-free interest rate;
   dS_t = Change in stock price over time interval dt;
   dt = Small time interval;
   σ_S = Volatility of the stock price;
   W_t = Brownian motion, which is a stochastic process characterised by normally distributed intervals dt with a mean of 0 and a variance equal to the length of the interval dt. Mathematically stated, the intervals dt have a distribution equal to $N(0, dt)$;
   dW_t = A stochastic process with distribution $N(0, dt)$.

For the purpose of understanding a quanto option a similar model to equation (12.1) is required which includes two additional variables – namely the correlation ρ between the logarithm of the stock price and the logarithm of the exchange rate and the FX volatility σ_{FX}. However, it is important to realize that this equation

---

[2] Assuming a share price movement according to equation (12.1) one can prove that the price of a call option on such a share is given by formula (2.1) and of a put option by formula (2.2).

defines a new share F_t quoted in the currency the option is quantoed into rather than the share's own currency. F_t is defined in such a way that a regular dollar option on F_t is in fact a quanto option on S_t:

$$\frac{dF_t}{F_t} = (r_{local} - \rho\sigma_S\sigma_{FX})\, dt + \sigma_S\, dW_t \qquad (12.2)$$

where $\quad \rho =$ Correlation between the logarithm of the stock price and the logarithm of the exchange rate, where the exchange rate is quoted as number of dollars per pound. A positive correlation means that if the pound increases in value the stock price goes up;

$r_{local} =$ Risk-free interest rate of the stock's own currency. In BP's case r_{local} is the risk-free interest rate of the pound.

From this equation it is obvious that anyone who holds a quanto call option benefits if the correlation decreases and the holder of a quanto put benefits if the correlation increases. Depending on the sign of the correlation this formula also makes clear whether the holder of a quanto option is long or short FX volatility. If the correlation is negative the holder of a quanto call is long FX volatility and the holder of a quanto put is short FX volatility. If the correlation is positive the holder of a quanto call is short FX volatility and the holder of a quanto put is long FX volatility. Knowing that the model for the change in stock price for a USD stock with a dividend yield equal to d is

$$\frac{dF_t}{F_t} = (r_\$ - d)\, dt + \sigma_S\, dW_t \qquad (12.3)$$

shows that the price of a quanto option can be derived from a normal option by making an adjustment to the dividend yield of adding $r_\$ - r_{local} + \rho\sigma_S\sigma_{FX}$ to the dividend yield. In equation (12.3) $r_\$$ is the USD risk-free interest rate.

12.2   THE COMPOSITE OPTION

The composite option is designed for investors who want to execute an option strategy on a foreign stock but want to fix the strike in their own currency and get the payout of this option in their own currency. In contrast to the quanto option, where the holder gets a percentage return regardless the exchange rate, the holder of a composite option has exposure to the exchange rate. One of the reasons that a composite option is traded is to protect the value in their own currency on a foreign investment. Consider the following example. A U.S. investor owns stock in the British pharmaceutical GlaxoSmithKline (GSK). Assume that the current value of GSK is £13.00 and that the exchange rate is $2 per pound. This means that the dollar value of one share is $26. To protect this holding he buys a 1-year at-the-money composite put option on GSK. This means that the strike price of this composite put option is equal to $26. Assume that after 1 year the stock goes down to £11.00 and the exchange rate goes from $2 per pound to $1.5 per pound (dollar increases in value). This means that the dollar value of one GSK share has gone down from $26 to $16.5. However, because the strike price of the composite option is fixed in dollars, the dollar loss on the shares will be offset by the payout of the composite put option, which is equal to the strike price ($26) minus the new dollar value of one GSK share ($16.5). In summary, the holder of a composite option wants to protect the share value in his own currency from both exchange rate movements as well as movements in the stock price.

The best way to answer the question whether the holder of a composite option is short or long correlation is to model the change in stock price, for a small time interval, in the currency of the composite. In the example above this would be the dollar. Using the same notation as in Section 12.1 the model looks as follows (see Appendix B):

$$\frac{dF_t}{F_t} = r_{compo} \, dt + \sigma_{compo} \, dW_t \qquad (12.4)$$

where

$$\sigma^2_{compo} = \sigma^2_S + 2\rho\sigma_S\sigma_{FX} + \sigma^2_{FX} \qquad (12.5)$$

and r_{compo} is the risk-free interest rate of the composite currency.

This formula shows that the holder of a composite option is long correlation.

Chapter
13

....

REPO

Ⅰn Section 1.3 it was mentioned that an investor is able to short stock he does not own. However, this principle where the investor borrows stock to subsequently short it comes at a certain cost and is often referred to as 'repo'.[1] Repo stands for 'repurchase agreement' and means that the lender agrees to sell the stock with the agreement to buy it back at a specified price[2] somewhere in the future. The lender always has the right to call the stock back.

In this chapter the definition of repo will be discussed, as will be its implications to the option market.

13.1   A REPO EXAMPLE

Consider an investor who is bearish (negative) on the stock Ahold. In this case he could short the stock Ahold at the prevailing market price, in which case he will benefit if Ahold decreases in value. However, for this strategy he would have to borrow the stock which would come at a certain cost. This cost is usually around 10 basis points (bps)[3] a year of the notional borrowed, if it is an easy borrow in which case it is referred to as 'general collateral' (gc).

---

[1] Although repo is seen as the cost of borrowing a stock this is not totally correct. The cost of borrowing a stock is really the difference between Libor and the repo rate, since the repo rate is less than Libor.

[2] This specified price is larger than what the lender sold the stock for initially and can be calculated by multiplying $(1 + \text{Repo rate})$ and the initial stock price.

[3] 1 basis point is $\frac{1}{100}$ of 1%.

Suppose the investor decides to short 100,000 shares of Ahold at \$10. If the lender charges him 10 bps per year, it would cost him \$1,000 ($\frac{1,000,000}{10,000} \times 10$) a year to have this position on.

This is just a simplified example of the mechanics of repo. In reality, there is a very sophisticated repo market to borrow and lend stocks. This means that the repo is never fixed and will depend on demand from borrowers and supply of lenders.

13.2 REPO IN CASE OF A TAKEOVER

A takeover usually has a positive impact on the share price of the takeover target and a negative impact on the share price of the acquiring company. The reason for this is that the acquiring company expects to get synergies and cost savings from this takeover and is therefore willing to pay a premium to the current share price of the takeover target. Because there are usually a few companies looking at the same takeover target, the premium paid over the current share price is usually so much that it only pays back when all the theoretical synergies and cost savings work out. This means that if something unexpected happens the acquiring company is likely to lose on the deal.[4] For this reason a takeover tends to

------

[4] This does not mean that every takeover is a bad deal. Very often, companies have to make takeovers in order to cut costs, which is necessary to survive amid fierce competition.

attract short players of the stock of the acquiring company, which pushes up the repo of this stock. In takeover situations one can see repo rates as high as 10% a year.

13.3   REPO AND ITS EFFECT ON OPTIONS

Dividends and repo rates have the same effect on the forward. In both cases a higher dividend or repo brings the forward down. This also means that repo rates can have a substantial impact on option prices.

If a stock's repo increases to particularly high levels, put options will become more expensive and call options less expensive. The reason becomes apparent when one looks at the different ways calls and puts are being hedged. If a trader buys a call option he will have to sell shares to hedge himself. In case of a high repo on a stock it would cost him a lot to put his hedge on because, if he wants to short the stock, he would have to borrow it at a very high rate. Since he only wants to pay a certain implied volatility he needs to lower the price of the call compared with a situation where there is a much lower repo. For a put option the reverse holds. If a trader buys a put he will buy the underlying stock to hedge himself. If this stock has a very high repo the investor can lend these shares and make additional money by doing so. Therefore, he can pay a higher premium and still get the same implied volatility compared with a situation where the underlying is treated as general collateral.

13.4 TAKEOVER IN CASH AND ITS EFFECT ON THE FORWARD

When a company is taken over in cash, this has a big impact on the prices of the options on this company. The reason is that, when a cash offer is submitted and accepted by shareholders, one can reasonably expect that the share price of the takeover target will no longer move and, more importantly, the forward changes significantly. As an example, consider the cash bid by Telefónica on O_2 for 200 pence per share. Suppose that the shares of O_2 will continue trading for another 3 months after Telefónica's offer has been made public, after which the shares will be delisted and the shareholders will receive 200 pence per share in cash. The question is obviously: What effect does this cash offer have on the price of a 2-year call option on O_2? To answer this question one first has to realize that the volatility of O_2 is next to 0. The next step is to think about what happens to the forward of O_2. Since O_2 shares will be delisted in 3 months a 2-year forward is equal to a 3-month forward. Since any forward longer than 3 months is equal to the 3-month forward, one can easily misprice call and put options with maturities over 3 months, especially if there is a big difference between the dividend yield and the risk-free interest rate. Knowing this, it is relatively easy to price a 2-year call option on O_2 with a strike price of 180 pence. Assuming O_2 will not pay any dividends, this call can be priced using equation (3.8), which expresses the price of a call in terms of its volatility and the forward. Since the stock will be delisted after 3 months the maturity $(T - t)$ of the call should be taken to be 3 months. Since the share price is higher than the strike price of 180 and the volatility is next to 0, d_1 in equation (3.8) is ∞ and, therefore, $N(d_1)$ and $N(d_2)$ are equal to 1. Plugging in all these variables into equation (3.8) gives a call price of $S_t - e^{-r(T-t)}K$,[5] where $T - t$ is 3 months. This price can be made intuitive by going back to how an option on an underlying with zero volatility and a maturity of 3 months is hedged. Since the share price is 200 pence, the strike price is 180 and the volatility is 0, the delta of the option is 1. So, if an investor buys the call he will hedge himself by selling the shares at 200 pence, S_t. The call will give the investor the right to buy the shares at 180 in 3 months' time. For this reason the value of the investor's portfolio will be $S_t e^{r(T-t)} - K$ in 3 months' time. Since the price of the call option is equal to the present value of the portfolio's value in 3 months' time, the call is worth $\left(S_t e^{r(T-t)} - K\right) e^{-r(T-t)} = S_t - e^{-r(T-t)}K$. By the same argument the value of an out-of-the-money call on O_2 should theoretically be 0.[6]

---

[5] This price holds if the options are closed out at intrinsic. In some cases the option exchange will compensate for the time value.
[6] In practice, an out-of-the-money call on a share on which a cash offer has been submitted will not be 0 because people will speculate on a counter offer.

Appendix

A

....

PROBABILITY THAT AN OPTION EXPIRES IN THE MONEY

Whenever the stock price movement is only known up to time t and the price at time t is S_t, the Black–Scholes formula gives that:

$$S_T = S_t\, e^{(r-\frac{1}{2}\sigma^2)(T-t)+\sigma y} \qquad (A.1)$$

provided it is a non-dividend paying stock. In the above formula y is normally distributed with mean 0 and variance 1. Now it is easy to calculate the probability that an option expires in the money. Take a call option. A call option expires in the money when $S_T > K$, where K is the strike price. This means:

$$S_T = S_t\, e^{(r-\frac{1}{2}\sigma^2)(T-t)+\sigma y} > K$$

$$\Updownarrow$$

$$y > -\frac{\ln\left(\dfrac{S_t}{K}\right) + \left(r - \frac{1}{2}\sigma^2\right)(T-t)}{\sigma\sqrt{T-t}}$$

$$= -d_2$$

Since y has a standard normal distribution:

$$P(\text{call expires in the money}) = P(S_T > K) = N(d_2)$$
$$(A.2)$$

In the same way one can derive:

$$P(\text{put expires in the money}) = P(S_T < K) = N(-d_2).$$
$$(A.3)$$

Appendix

B

....

VARIANCE OF A COMPOSITE OPTION

I t is very easy to prove that the variance of a composite option is equal to:

$$\sigma_{compo}^2 = \sigma_S^2 + 2\rho\sigma_S\sigma_{FX} + \sigma_{FX}^2 \qquad (B.2)$$

One just has to compare the movement of the underlying in the composite currency with the movement of a geometric basket option composed of the underlying in the local currency and the FX rate. The formula for this basket option is as follows:

$$F_t = S_{t,local}S_{t,FX} \qquad (B.2)$$

where

$$\frac{dS_{t,local}}{S_{t,local}} = r_{local}\,dt + \sigma_S\,dW_{1,t} \qquad (B.2)$$

and[1]

$$\frac{dS_{t,FX}}{S_{t,FX}} = \left(r_{compo} - r_{local}\right)dt + \sigma_{FX}\,dW_{2,t} \qquad (B.3)$$

Since

$$Var[\ln(F_t)] = Var\left[\ln\left(S_{t,local}S_{t,FX}\right)\right]$$

$$= Var\left[\ln\left(S_{t,local}\right)\right) + \ln\left(S_{t,FX}\right)\right]$$

$$= \left(\sigma_S^2 + 2\rho\sigma_S\sigma_{FX} + \sigma_{FX}^2\right)t \qquad (B.4)$$

---

[1] To get an intuition for equation (B.3), imagine an exchange rate with zero volatility, and therefore the value of the exchange rate only changes because of differences in risk-free interest rates between the currencies. In this case $S_{t+dt,FX} = S_{t,FX} \cdot \dfrac{1 + r_{compo}\,dt}{1 + r_{local}\,dt}$. Taylor expansion gives that this is equal to $S_{t,FX}\left(1 + \left(r_{compo} - r_{local}\right)dt\right)$.

and

$$E[\ln(F_t)] = E\left[\ln\left(S_{t,local}S_{t,FX}\right)\right] \qquad (B.5)$$

$$= r_{local}t + \left(r_{compo} - r_{local}\right)t \qquad (B.6)$$

$$= r_{compo}t \qquad (B.7)$$

the movement of the stock in the composite currency can be modelled according to equation (12.4).

BIBLIOGRAPHY

Aarts, P. (1999). Pricing the basket option and exploring its volatility structure. Mathematics thesis, Utrecht University, Utrecht, The Netherlands.

Durrett, R. (1996). *Probability: Theory and Examples*, 2nd edn. Duxbury Press, Belmont, California.

Grimmett, G.R. and D.R. Stirzaker (1992). *Probability and Random Processes*, 2nd edn. Clarendon Press, Oxford, UK.

Hull, J.C. (1993). *Options, Futures, and Other Derivative Securities*, 2nd edn. Prentice Hall, Englewood Cliffs, New Jersey.

Hull, J.C. (1997). *Options, Futures and Other Derivatives*, Prentice Hall, Englewood Cliffs, New Jersey.

Lamberton, D. and B. Lapeyre (1996). *Introduction to Stochastic Calculus Applied to Finance*, Chapman & Hall, London.

Roelfsema, M.R. (2000). *Exploiting the Dependencies between Index and Stock Options*. Delft University Press, Delft, The Netherlands.

Weert, F.J. (2002). Basket en skew arbitrage. Mathematics thesis, Utrecht University, Utrecht, The Netherlands.

Wilmott, P. (1998). *Derivatives: The Theory and Practice of Financial Engineering*, university edn. John Wiley & Sons, Chichester, UK.

INDEX

· ·